BLACKSTONE'S PREPARING FOR POLICE DUTY

BLACKSTONE'S PREPARING FOR POLICE DUTY

FRASER SAMPSON

OXFORD
UNIVERSITY PRESS

OXFORD

UNIVERSITY PRESS

Great Clarendon Street, Oxford OX2 6DP

Oxford University Press is a department of the University of Oxford.
It furthers the University's objective of excellence in research, scholarship,
and education by publishing worldwide in

Oxford New York

HV8196
A2
535
2003

Auckland Bangkok Buenos Aires Cape Town Chennai
Dar es Salaam Delhi Hong Kong Istanbul Karachi Kolkata
Kuala Lumpur Madrid Melbourne Mexico City Mumbai Nairobi
São Paulo Shanghai Taipei Tokyo Toronto

Oxford is a registered trade mark of Oxford University Press
in the UK and in certain other countries

Published in the United States
by Oxford University Press Inc., New York

0 4955227 9

British Library Cataloguing in Publication Data
Data available

Library of Congress Cataloging in Publication Data
Data available

ISBN 0-19-925556-3

3 5 7 9 10 8 6 4 2

Typeset by RefineCatch Limited, Bungay, Suffolk
Printed in Great Britain by Biddles Ltd, King's Lynn, Norfolk

CONTENTS

DETAILED CONTENTS

FOREWORD

The public expectations of police officers are high, and the operational demands are many and generally challenging. New recruits—or constables in their probationary period—have to master a comprehensive range of knowledge and skills, and quickly learn the attitudes and behaviours necessary to gain and maintain public confidence, and to do the job competently and professionally. They need all the help and support they can get at the start of their careers!

Fraser Sampson had nearly 20 years service as a police officer both on the front line, and in training at the force level and nationally. To this book, which commendably aims to help potential recruits and probationer constables to use their time profitably, he brings a wealth of experience, and a passion for learning.

Having conducted a major thematic inspection of police probationer training in 2001, and produced the report *Training Matters* (which is referred to in the book), I know how important it is to make learning accessible, easy to understand, and attractive. This book is a welcome contribution, and I commend it to the reader.

RA Field-Smith MBE MA FCIPD FCMI
HM Inspector of Police Training
Surrey

INTRODUCTION

Policing is a complicated business—and it's getting more complicated all the time. Over the past ten years policing within England and Wales has changed dramatically and will change even further over the next decade.

Imagine for a moment that you are a visitor to London. You see two uniformed officers on the street speaking to a member of the public. Nothing unusual or complicated in that. You would probably assume that the officers were constables in the Metropolitan Police Service, the largest police force in Great Britain and the one responsible for policing most of London. But they might equally be constables in the City of London police, responsible for policing the 'square mile', or they could be from the British Transport Police, a national police force who police not only the London Underground system, but also the entire railway network. All of these are 'regular' police officers whose uniform is generally identical. Alternatively, the officers might be constables in the Royal Parks Police, or they might be Special Constables in any of the above forces. Recent changes in policing mean that one or both officers might not be police officers at all but Community Support Officers or specially accredited security staff.

In addition to the two officers in the scenario above, there will also be a great many other people who, though unseen, are playing a vital part in the interaction that is taking place on the street: communications staff and computer operators at the other end of the officers' radios for instance. Putting an effective police officer or auxiliary on the street requires a huge network of other professionals such as personnel and administrative staff, supervisors and managers, mechanics and technicians, investigators, scene examiners—the list goes on and on. Each of these roles and the complex infrastructure that surrounds them is critical to effective policing operations in any particular area.

As well as becoming more complicated, policing is also becoming more important to the everyday lives of the people in our communities.

In a recent debate in the House of Lords on the Police Reform Bill, former Commissioner of the Metropolitan Police, Lord Condon pointed out that:

Police officers can intervene in people's lives in a way that alters those lives forever—for good or for evil.

This observation is true, not only of England and Wales, but every country and every jurisdiction in the world. And it isn't just *police officers* who can intervene in people's lives in this way; the same can be said of anyone who has been entrusted with carrying out police duties. This extends way beyond sworn police officers and includes the whole extended 'police family', encompassing special constables, support officers and auxiliary staff in all their forms.

Policing in this broader sense has become so complex that understanding how it all works is a challenge in itself. At the same time, policing activity can have such an impact on our lives that it has become one of the key elements determining quality of life within a regional, community or even a family setting.

Those who take part in policing at any level are therefore entrusted with playing a significant role in the lives of others, and presented with an unparalleled challenge. Preparing for those roles and challenges demands a lot. There is no such thing as an easy policing job. As well as the key motivational factors, physical attributes and potential for development, effective, efficient and professional policing requires effective, efficient and professional training. While much of that training will be designed and delivered in a variety of ways using many different media, there are some fundamental issues behind police duties that can be addressed at a very early stage in a book such as this.

So, whether you have been through the recruit assessment process for appointment as a police constable, are undergoing training in a support or auxiliary role or if you are still considering your options generally, this book is intended to help you.

There are limits on the depth and breadth that can be covered in a book of this nature. At different stages—particularly in Part III—you will come across boxed text headed 'Attention to Detail'. These are designed to prompt more detailed thinking in some key areas. For the very enthusiastic, further questions of detail to test your understanding more fully can be found on the website at the end of Chapter 1.

Setting out how policing is organised in England and Wales, looking at who does what, how and why, this book introduces the 'policing landscape' before going on to consider some key areas of police law and procedure, as well as unravelling some of the mysteries involved in preparing for police duty.

PART I
THE POLICE AND POLICING

1

WHO DOES IT?

A good place to start is generally the beginning, but tracking the source of organised policing in England and Wales is hard to do with any accuracy. Although the appointment of people with special powers to arrest and punish offenders can be traced right back as far as the 14th century, it's not really until around 1800 that you can find a full-time police force in the history books. By 1829, the then Home Secretary Sir Robert Peel had created the Metropolitan Police comprising some 3,000 officers to police England's capital city. After this time, other police forces beyond London were formed and, in 1964, the current arrangement of 43 police forces covering England and Wales was put in place.

The policing landscape

There are 43 'local' police forces covering the various counties and regions that link up England and Wales; there are also some specialist police forces such as the Ministry of Defence police, the UK Atomic Energy Authority police and the British Transport Police. Governing the management of all police forces is what is often called the tripartite system. This is made up of the chief officer, the police authority and the Home Office. Each has a distinct and shared role in the management, direction and funding of the police. As Home Secretary David Blunkett (jokingly) put it, 'one has all the power, one has all the money and the other gets all the blame'. The 43 regional forces are often referred to as Home Office police forces (and the others 'non-Home Office'). Some of the

43 Home Office forces have the same name as the county they police—
West Yorkshire, Cumbria and Essex are good examples. Confusingly,
others cover several counties or areas which have different names—
examples of these would be Thames Valley, West Mercia and South Wales.
More confusingly, some forces put 'Constabulary' after their name, while
others just call themselves 'Police'. As for London, the policing of the
capital still falls to the Metropolitan Police Service, along with the City
of London police who, as discussed above, police the 'square mile'.

Figure 1.1   Forces map

Source: The Association of Police Authorities

Each of the 43 forces has its own PNC reporting number. This is a nationally recognised numbering system used by the Police National Computer and helps to identify officers and vehicles from certain forces, particularly when they are used in joint operations.

The 43 police forces are made up of around 130,000 officers—a record number amounting to about one police officer for every 400 people in the community. Not surprisingly, the larger forces are centred around those areas with the largest populations such as London, the West Midlands and Greater Manchester. Each police force has a Chief Officer in charge—in the Metropolitan Police and the City of London police this person holds the rank of Commissioner; in the other forces they hold the rank of Chief Constable. The Chief Officer is responsible for the day-to-day management of his or her force and for policing operations carried out within that particular region. At the moment there is only one way of entering the police forces of England and Wales—and that is in the rank of constable. All police officers begin their career as probationary constables and most have to complete a two-year probation before being confirmed in the role.

The badges for each rank are shown on p 10. Although there are some special career paths for some fast-track entrants (see the Higher Potential Development and Graduate Entry Schemes) all police officers have to pass the sergeants' examination before they can be promoted above the rank of constable. After that they will have to pass the inspectors' examination before moving on further. Both examinations are designed to test officers' knowledge and, just as importantly, their practical skills to see whether they can really *do* the job. The written part of the examination is a multiple-choice question paper on law and procedure, followed six months later by an assessment centre which tests the relevant skills required for the rank. The examinations, known as OSPRE (Objective Structured Performance Related Examination), are held once a year and are based around the behaviours (or competencies) that are discussed in greater detail in Chapter 3.

Figure 1.2   Rank badges

Source: The Metropolitan Police Service

Policing areas are generally broken down into Divisions, each having a senior officer in charge. These Divisions are made up of one or more police stations whose activities and policing operations can be adapted and directed according to the local needs of the immediate communities. Many large Divisions have headquarters that are referred to as Basic Command Units or BCUs.

The Metropolitan Police service is the largest single police force in England and Wales. Its headquarters is probably one of the most well-known police addresses in the world—New Scotland Yard. The Metropolitan Police district is divided into five areas, each of which is about the same size as an average provincial police force. Some of the ranks within the Metropolitan Police service and the City of London police are slightly different from those in the other forces in England and Wales.

The police family

In addition to the police officers themselves (who hold 'the office of constable'—see below), effective policing requires a whole range of other skills and abilities. All police forces depend heavily on their support staff, formerly referred to as civilians. These police staff are essential to the administration and the management of all police organisations. Not only do police staff provide key services in relation to administration, personnel and training functions, they also provide vital operational skills in the areas of communications, IT, Crime Scene Examination, fingerprint and crime pattern analysis and beyond.

In addition, the Police Reform Act 2002 has created the opportunity to train people in a number of new policing roles and to give them, for the first time, a range of police powers. Some of these officers are employed by the relevant police force while others are employed by other bodies such as local authorities or private organisations and are 'accredited' by the chief officer of police for that area. There are also literally tens of thousands of local street wardens, neighbourhood watch volunteers and others who support the work of the police and other agencies.

Let us take a closer look at some of these extended police family members.

Police staff

Police staff are very much a part of the police family and their role has become increasingly important—and increasingly varied. Each of the many support roles can offer its own challenging and rewarding policing career path, either for people who want to get involved in policing but don't want to become police constables—as regular or Special Constables—or as an entry point for people who wish to develop their competence to the level required of police recruits.

Sworn police constables

For those who *do* want to be sworn in as police officers there are also many specialised areas of work. These include:

- uniformed patrol
- community safety
- custody officers
- domestic and family violence
- firearms
- police dogs
- underwater search teams.

Included among the ranks of fully sworn or 'attested' police officers are Special Constables.

Special constables

As their name says, Special Constables are sworn holders of the office of constable (as discussed in Chapter 2). 'Specials' receive comprehensive training and wear police uniform. When acting in their own force area— or a neighbouring force area—Specials have all the powers of other police constables. Their duties typically involve patrolling busy areas at times of high activity such as weekends and evenings, and also carrying out front-line operational duties at major events such as sports fixtures, conferences and other public attractions. There are currently around 13,000 Special Constables in England and Wales (and at one time there were over 140,000!). The contribution to policing made by Specials has become more widely recognised and appreciated in recent years and many police forces, along with the Home Office, are keen to see more Specials recruited and trained. In a recent debate in the House of Commons, Specials were described in this way: 'the beauty of Special Constables is that they are properly trained, genuine, 100% police officers' (*Hansard*, 27 June 2002).

Recently, eight police forces set out to spearhead a drive to recruit more Specials and to spread good practice in using them to best effect. There forces are:

* Merseyside
* West Midlands
* Greater Manchester
* Kent
* Surrey
* South Yorkshire
* Norfolk and
* South Wales.

In the first ever National Policing Plan, the Home Secretary has said that Specials have 'an important role to play in reducing crime and providing reassurance to the public'. He goes on to say how their work both 'encourages community cohesion and helps the police service to reflect the communities they serve'.

Further details about the work of the Special Constabulary can be found on the Home Office website, listed at the end of this chapter.

Citizens in uniform

One feature that is shared by *all* sworn constables is that they are citizens in uniform. There are some very wide ranging powers that are given to police officers once they have been sworn in as a constable (see below) and, if you choose to join the police in that role, you will be entrusted with those powers. Those who join the police in other roles may also be entrusted with legal powers, albeit not as extensive as those of sworn constables, but nevertheless requiring a high standard of training and responsibility in their use.

However, it is important to remember that as constables or auxiliaries, you will still, first and foremost, be members of your community. Although there are some police duties that involve confrontation with some individuals, policing does not mean that you have to become isolated from your community; quite the reverse. The very first police officers in England and Wales *wanted* to be seen as simply 'citizens in uniform' and those uniforms were designed so that the officers looked as much like ordinary members of the community as possible.

This idea of *citizens in uniform* is an important feature to remember. The people who police our communities are drawn from ordinary members of those communities—much like juries who are used in the trial of some serious criminal offences. That is why it is important that the police service reflects the community in terms of representation of

—

all ethnic and racial groups, and both sexes. For this reason the police have put a great deal of energy and effort into encouraging women and people from minority ethnic backgrounds to apply for jobs. As a result there are now over 20,000 female police officers and more than 2,300 police officers from minority backgrounds.

The table below, produced from Home Office statistics, shows the make up of the police service in England and Wales as at 31 March 2002.

Rank	Male	Female	Total	% age Female
Chief Constable	47	6	53	11
Assistant CC	141	10	151	7
Super/C Super	1173	83	1256	7
C/Insp	1433	117	1550	8
Insp	57171	479	6195	8
Sergeant	16621	1953	18574	20
Constable	104483	22784	127267	18

These figures are rounded to the nearest whole number and account for full-time officers (excluding those seconded to other agencies).

Of these officers, 3,386 declared themselves as being from visible minority ethnic backgrounds—amounting to 2.6% of the overall strength and an increase of 14% over the previous year.

At the time the statistics were compiled, there were 58,909 full-time police staff in support roles, over 60% of whom were female.

In the first ever National Policing Plan, the government has set out its target of achieving a fully 'representative' police service by 2009. In 2001, around 30% of all police recruits were women and changes to working and training conditions mean that more women are likely to be attracted to a policing role in the future. While it is true that all police officers and auxiliary personnel have put themselves forward to take on extra responsibility within the community and to be trained to do so, like you they and their families are still members of the communities in which they live, learn and work.

Many people within the police service of England and Wales have worked hard towards gaining and retaining the confidence of minority groups. While the effort that some individuals and organisations have invested in this key area of community policing is unarguable, there is still a fair way to go. As HM Chief Inspector of Constabulary Sir Keith Povey QPM put it recently in the Report *Diversity Matters*, 2003:

> *Policing in England and Wales takes place with the consent of the public, all of the public. This is not something that can be taken for granted. The public must have confidence in the police service if their consent is to be sustained. Fair and equitable treatment, by police officers and police staff, of every member of the community, irrespective of any aspect of diversity, is essential if public support is to be maintained. Futhermore, if the police service is to attract the workforce it requires in the future, this concept of respect for all aspects of diversity must extend to the impartial treatment of colleagues.*

Uniformed patrol—the front rank

Central to every police force in England and Wales is the uniformed patrolled officer. First on the scene of almost every incident, these officers have to be prepared to deal with any eventuality. Whether dealing with a domestic dispute or a suspicious death, a burglary, street robbery or shoplifter, a pub fight or a train crash, it is usually the uniformed patrolled officers who will be called first.

Any experienced police officer will tell you it is the things that are done—or not done—during the first minutes of an incident being reported that are often the most important. Even in major investigations such as murders, abductions and terrorist incidents the actions of the first officers on the scene are critical. And the person that is usually in the best position to make sure the right things are done in these vital moments is the uniformed patrol officer.

The presence of uniformed patrols on the street can have a big effect within a community. Not only can they deter crime, making an area safer but, just as importantly, their presence makes people *feel* safer.

Of all police personnel, uniformed patrol officers are the closest to the public. Whether serving in inner cities, towns or rural areas, they—assisted by their support staff—are the eyes and ears of the force and their knowledge of people, places and practices is invaluable.

For many police officers, uniformed patrol work represents the very reason why they joined the police in the first place. Take a look at some of the comments from operational officers in Chapter 2. Sharp-end, front line policing with all its challenges, excitements and rewards (as well as its frustrations) is what they joined to do—and many carry on doing it for their whole careers.

Specialist roles and departments

The need for greater flexibility in policing has meant that fewer and fewer officers work in separate specialist areas. Patrol officers increasingly do some work in plain clothes for instance, while some detectives are now issued with uniforms. However, for those who want to specialise beyond patrol, there are still many different areas to choose from. A few examples are set out below.

Tutor constables

One of the most important roles in the development of newly-recruited police officers is that of the tutor. Drawn from experienced and high performing front line officers, tutor constables work alongside their probationary colleagues, ensuring that those colleagues receive the right level of on-the-job support, guidance and direction that they need in order to develop their skills competently and confidently. Tutor constables are an essential part of a police officer's initial training and their importance has received a great deal of recognition and praise in a number of different forums.

The tutor's role is probably the most valuable and influential in the experiential learning process. This process is explained in greater detail in Chapter 5. As well as providing careful guidance, reassurance and a professional presence to stop any wheels coming off, the tutor is there to maximise the learning and development that you as a probationary police officer get from your early operational experience.

Road traffic

The enforcement of some traffic laws such as speed limits, heavy goods vehicles and passenger vehicles requires specialist knowledge and training. So too does the examination of vehicles and the investigation of accidents—particularly where someone has been killed.

For this reason, officers who are specially training in the relevant law and procedure—as well as in advanced driving skills—are used in road traffic departments by most, if not all forces in England and Wales. The Police Reform Act 2002 also allows for some road traffic duties—such as escorting wide-load vehicles—to be carried out by auxiliary staff.

Criminal investigation

Although the prevention and detection of crime is a primary responsibility of all police officers, there are some investigations that require additional specialist training and experience. Gathering intelligence and evidence is a vital part of the police role in tackling crime and again sometimes calls for particular skills—from police officers and civilian support staff alike. These skills can be found, not only in detectives and investigators, but also in roles such as crime scene visitors, fingerprint analysts and technical support.

Changing roles in policing mean that the traditional idea of the Criminal Investigation Department (CID) detective is also changing. However, although the way in which forces use them varies widely, the trained detective is a very valuable resource and, according to Home Office figures, they make up about one in eight police officers. The Police Reform Act 2002 allows for the recruitment and training of Investigation Officers who will help detectives and other crime investigators in the interviewing of prisoners, searching of premises and gathering of evidence.

Some police forces have other specific areas of specialisation (e.g. air support units). Given its size and the nature of its work, the Metropolitan Police service has a great many other units and departments to which officers may be posted or attached.

There are also a number of organisations outside the 43 police forces themselves which employ officers on secondment, as well as civilian staff and investigators from other backgrounds. Examples of these are:

- The National Crime Squad (NCS)—dealing with the investigation of serious and organised crime on a regional and national basis. In the future it will be possible for police officers to join the NCS directly, rather than being seconded from their parent forces as they are at the moment.

- The National Criminal Intelligence Service (NCIS)—dealing with the collection and monitoring of intelligence of crime and criminals and being staffed by many investigative agencies including HM Customs and Excise. As with the NCS above, NCIS will soon be able to recruit police officers directly.

- The Central Police Training and Development Authority (CPTDA). Working under the much easier name of Centrex, the CPTDA has responsibility for many aspects of police training and development. In addition to overseeing the design and delivery of probationer training, investigators' training and other key areas, Centrex is also responsible for evaluating police training to see if it actually works; they also set the national police promotion exams, probationer development tests and advise on the assessment of recruits. Centrex is staffed by a mixture of non-police personnel and seconded police officers.

WEBSITES

→ www.police.uk
→ www.policecouldyou.com
→ www.policetraining.com
→ www.homeoffice.gov.uk
→ www.ncis.co.uk
→ www.pito.org.uk
→ www.detail-technologies.co.uk

FURTHER READING

Blackstone's Police Manuals, 2003/4, Oxford: OUP.
The National Policing Plan 2003–2006, Home Office.
Home Office Circulars 23–25 of 2002.
The Police Promotion Examinations Syllabus—The Employers' Organisation, London.
Policing a New Century: a Blueprint for Reform (CM5326) 2001, HMSO.
Wall, *The Chief Constables of England and Wales*, 1998, Dartmouth.
Reiner, *The Politics of the Police*, 3rd edn, 2000, Oxford: OUP.
The Future of Multi-ethnic Britain—The Parekh Report, 2000, London: Profile Books (The Runnymede Trust).

2

PREPARING FOR WHAT?

Policing is an extraordinary job done by extraordinary people. The constant and unrelenting nature of policing means that the job never stops—not for public holidays, religious holidays, World Cup football matches, New Year celebrations, day or night. In fact many of its challenges come at times when others are playing, partying, protesting; marrying, moving and mourning. That's not to say that police officers and support staff don't get to have their own home and private lives—they enjoy generous entitlement for time off and very flexible working conditions. But the job goes on, and sometimes it can make quite heavy demands.

There is huge variety in the roles that keep the job going. From uniformed patrol officers to civilian crime analysts, crime investigators to scenes of crime examiners, special branch to mounted branch, traffic patrols to traffic wardens, IT specialists, HR specialists, search teams, firearms teams and child protection teams—they all play a vital part in the policing of the community and the community of policing.

Similarly, there is enormous variety in the make up of the community—or communities—that need to be policed. The cultural, ethnic and social diversity in England and Wales is something that is both considered, and where possible, reflected, by the police service. During their initial and career-long training, police personnel are encouraged to consider the particular needs of sections of their community, sections such as asylum seekers, people with disabilities, travellers and transgender/transsexuals.

A question that a lot of people want to ask of police officers and some of their civilian colleagues is: 'Why do you do it?' Here are some of their answers to that question:

> ... *to gain experience of good and bad parts of life and see things the public will rarely see.* (Police Constable, 16 months' service)

> ... *fed up with office job in which I felt I was achieving nothing.* (Police Sergeant, 7 years' service)

> ... *bored with the same thing every day. Want challenges and the support of colleagues.* (Police Constable, 1 year's service)

> ... *deal with a variety of incidents and gain satisfaction of helping the public.* (Police Constable, 10 months' service)

> ... *assisting people with their problems and being given the opportunity to help them—also the money isn't bad!* (Police Sergeant)

Police officers are often also asked: 'Having joined, what advice would you give a new recruit?'

> ... *give the service at least two years to see if the career is for you. Always keep an open mind and remember ... treat everybody with the same dignity.* (Police Sergeant, 6 years' service)

> ... *speak to serving police officers to get a real sense of the job.* (Police Constable, 2 years' service)

> ... *find out what the job actually entails as opposed to the image given by advertising campaigns or TV programmes.* (Police Constable, 9 months' service)

> ... *get some experience of life before joining. Be prepared for the selection process, don't give up trying—it's the best job I've ever had.* (Police Sergeant, 7 years' service)

Reassurance

Policing any community deals with a huge variety of things from controlling traffic to running complex investigations—and it is this variety of work that attracts a lot of people to the job. Whatever particular task they are involved in, the work of the police will be based on the needs of their community but there are certain key areas that lie at the heart of all police work. These are generally concerned with protecting people from crime, from the effects of crime and—often much harder to measure— from the *fear* of crime.

Among all the statistics about crime—how many offences are committed every minute, the likelihood of being burgled etc.—one of the most important things to consider is people's fear of crime. Sometimes this can be out of all proportion to the real situation—like people who worry that their plane will crash when flying away on holiday. The fact that by far the most dangerous part of their journey is the drive to the airport doesn't really help to calm these worries. Just think of the fear that the anthrax scares created in 2001—all of a sudden people were panicked by the presence of harmless white powders which had previously gone unnoticed. When you're frightened, statistics are not much comfort. Many such fears are irrational, but they're still real. Therefore, if people are worried about being burgled or raped, those fears are a real concern for them, the community and those who police it. On the other hand, there are many things that can *increase* people's fear of crime—things that might seem minor such as graffiti, litter and noise. If people in the community are genuinely scared to leave their homes or use public transport that is a real issue for the police and if vandalism, drunkenness and anti-social behaviour increase that fear, they too are important issues for policing.

So, while major investigations into serious and organised crime form a very important part of police duty, so too does tackling anti-social behaviour and maintaining a reassuring presence on the streets.

A brief look at your local newspaper or local TV news programmes will show you exactly what activity the police in your area are concerned with; it will also show you how far the work of the police touches the day-to-day lives of everyone. A good way to see for yourself how some of this work is planned is to go to community forums that are being held in your area—or any other venues where your local police are seeking community involvement. You can get details from your local police station.

Knowing and understanding what is going on in your community is a *vital* policing skill, possibly one of the most important of all. As Her Majesty's Inspector of Constabulary points out in *Training Matters* 2002:

> *Effective police officers are those that have a fundamental understanding of the environment in which they serve.*

Police constables

In Chapter 1, the concept of sworn constables was introduced. These are officers who, whether in the Special Constabulary or as full-time officers of the regular police service, have been sworn in as constables. Central to the whole policing system in England and Wales is what is called the *'office of constable'*. Although the title—and rank—of Police Constable is given to all police officers on joining the service (see Chapter 1), the slightly odd expression 'office of constable' goes much wider than that.

If you join the service as a police officer, at some point in your initial training you will be 'attested' or sworn in. This means that you make a sworn promise before a magistrate where you promise to carry out your duties as a police officer fairly and properly, according to the law. The oath is as follows:

> *I . . . . . of . . . . . do solemnly and sincerely declare and affirm that I will well and truly serve the Queen in the office of constable, with fairness, integrity, diligence and impartiality, upholding fundamental human rights and according equal respect to all people; and that I will, to the*

best of my power, cause the peace to be kept and preserved and prevent all offences against people and property; and that while I continue to hold the said office I will, to the best of my skill and knowledge, discharge all the duties thereof faithfully according to law.

Recruits in Wales have a Welsh language alternative as follows:

Rwyf i ... o ... yn datgan ac yn cadarnhau yn ddifrifol ac yn ddiffuant byddaf yn gwasanaethu'r Frenhines yn dda ac yn gywir yn fy swydd o heddwas (heddferch), yn deg, yn onest, yn ddiwyd ac yn ddiduedd, gan gynnal hawliau dynol sylfaenol a chan roddi'r un parch i bob person; ac y byddaf i, hyd eithaf fy ngallu, yn achosi i'r heddwch gael ei gadw a'i ddiogelu ac yn atal pob trosedd yn erbyn pobl ac eiddo; a thra byddaf yn parhau i ddal y swydd ddywededig y byddaf i, hyd eithaf fy sgil a'm gwybodaeth, yn cyflawni'r holl ddyletswyddau sy'n gysylltiedig â hi yn ffyddlon yn unol â'r gyfraith.

Once sworn in you receive a warrant card from your Chief Officer. From then on you will be regarded in law as holding 'the office of constable'.

As someone holding that position, you would not be an 'employee' of your particular police service in the way that you would be if you joined as a civilian investigator or member of auxiliary or support staff. For this reason you won't get a contract of employment as you might have done in a previous job. In effect you will have become the holder of a public office—a grand sounding title but also a fact of police life that has some important implications.

First, and most important, holding the office of constable means that you are given some specific powers that other citizens don't have. It's true that some other people have specific legal powers to do their job—people such as investigators, detention staff and others; it's also true that members of the public have certain basic powers to arrest people and prevent crime (see Chapter 8). However, the powers given to police officers (whatever their rank) are far wider than those given to any other law enforcement staff. These powers include the power to:

* stop vehicles
* control and direct traffic
* cordon off streets
* remove vehicles from roads
* issue fixed penalty notices
* enter premises
* search people, buildings and vehicles
* seize property, and, of course,
* to arrest people.

These powers are given to all police officers. Police officers holding higher ranks continue to be 'constables' and are given further powers such as the power to authorise a person's detention, to grant bail and to require certain types of searches or the taking of bodily samples.

Auxiliary and police staff

Policing is far too big a job to be left to sworn police officers alone. In spite of their extensive powers and training, police officers cannot carry out all the many tasks and roles associated with modern police services. As a result, the work of police constables is now supported by a growing number of auxiliary and police staff. In Chapter 1 you looked at the concept of the wider 'police family' and briefly saw a number of these other roles.

In order to make the most efficient and effective use of fully trained and sworn constables, police forces in the past have identified roles and responsibilities that can be—and perhaps should be—carried out by other staff. Generally those other staff have not been given any specific police powers and have been focused mainly on 'indoor' or non-patrolling functions. While these roles have proved very successful in supporting operational patrol officers and freeing them up to concentrate on the tasks that really require their full range of skills and powers, there has still been room for further expansion. The lack of police powers has, for instance, proved to be a hindrance in cases of detention officers and investigators, while there has also been a need to provide greater operational support in the form of patrol duties and tackling anti-social behaviour. As a result, chief officers have recently been given the option of employing auxiliary staff in much wider roles, roles that involve the use of certain police powers. While chief officers don't *have to* appoint any people in this way, many have shown an interest in doing so, particularly in larger urban areas such as London.

These auxiliary staff are appointed under the Police Reform Act 2002 and include:

- Community Support Officers. These officers help with patrol functions, maintaining order and tackling anti-social behaviour.

- Investigation Officers. These officers help with the investigation of crime, interviewing suspects, gathering and presenting evidence.

- Detention Officers. These officers work mainly within police stations, helping to process prisoners.

- Escort Officers. These officers help by escorting prisoners between police stations and also between different police areas.

Another support role created by the Police Reform Act 2002 is that of the 'accredited support officers'. Although not directly employed by a particular police force, people having this special accreditation are authorised by the local Chief Constable or Commissioner to use certain police powers. Examples of accredited people would be security staff at shopping malls and other privately-owned areas.

Whatever role they perform, all these auxiliary personnel will be given extensive training enabling them to do their job and, where relevant, uniforms or other badges of authority.

All of the above personnel can be granted certain specific police powers by the relevant chief officer of police in their area. These powers are discussed later in Chapter 8.

But whether you are a sworn police constable, an auxiliary police employee or anyone else entrusted with legal powers, there is one feature that is absolutely crucial to your role—discretion.

Discretion

Any police powers that are given to you are given to *you* as an individual. How, when and even *if* you choose to use these powers is a matter for your own discretion—which is why it's vitally important that you understand what they are.

If you are given policing powers, you will also be given training in the detail of what you can and can't do, what certain legal expressions mean and how they affect any powers you may have. These are essential elements of professional competence and a full understanding of the nature and extent of any powers is very important. But a further aspect of policing—probably the most important of all and the hardest to develop—is the use of discretion. This is also something that all police officers will learn about throughout their training, both in the classroom and on the street and it is the ability to use discretionary powers responsibly and effectively that makes experienced constables so valuable.

What is discretion? In his report into the disorders in Brixton in the early 1980s, Lord Scarman highlighted the importance of discretion for police officers. This very senior judge described discretion as the art of 'suiting action to circumstance'. In other words, it's matching the right course of action to the right situation; choosing the most appropriate response when faced with different scenarios.

While it is necessary to know the ingredients of any powers you might have been given, such as when you can demand a person's name and address or who you can search and when, the critical skill is learning whether to make that demand or carry out that search at all. Just because you have a power to do something does not meant that you *have* to use it. Like referees and umpires, teachers, parents and guardians, police officers are trusted with authority—and they are expected to use that authority sensibly and fairly. Often the best referees, teachers and parents are seen as being good at what they do because they do the right thing at the right time.

Understanding if and when you should use your police powers is as important as knowing what those powers are. Lord Scarman said that exercising discretion was the police officer's daily task—and that hasn't changed.

Conduct

Professionalism in policing doesn't just apply in the area of using—or *not* using—police powers. Holding the 'office of constable' also means that high standards of behaviour are expected of you—both on and off duty. For this reason, police officers are subject to a Code of Conduct. An extract from the Code puts it this way:

> The primary duties of those who hold the office of constable are the protection of life and property, the preservation of the Queen's peace, and the prevention and detection of criminal offences. To fulfil these duties they are granted extraordinary powers; the public and the police service therefore have the right to expect the highest standards of conduct from them.

You can find more on this Code of Conduct in Chapter 6.

There are similar requirements made of auxiliary staff, most of whom are in a different position from constables because they are 'employees' of their police force.

As well as the higher standard of conduct, being a police constable also brings with it some other restrictions on your personal life. Again, these are things that you might not expect—such as the fact that you cannot open a pub or join a trades union (although there are special rules if you are already a member of a union when you join the police). Taking those two as an example, these rules make sense when you realise, for instance, that the police have some specific duties in relation to liquor licensing and that they cannot bargain with employers in the way that 'employees' can. But it's not all one-way. Police officers are protected in their employment and cannot just be sacked by their chief officers. Also, alongside the restrictions on their lives, police officers enjoy the protection of the courts when carrying out their job in a proper manner. Many of the benefits within their pay and pension arrangements are also designed to reflect the extra responsibility they are taking on. Similarly, the fact that police officers cannot join unions does not mean that their welfare and working conditions are left unprotected; quite the opposite in fact. For a start, all police officers can join the Police Federation of England and Wales. The Federation is primarily responsible for looking after the welfare and efficiency of all police officers up to the rank of chief superintendent. There are also many other support groups and associations in place for police officers, such as the National Black Police Officers' Association, the British Women Police Officers' Association and the Gay Police Officers' Association. You will find the contact details for all these organisations at the end of this chapter.

So, being a constable is much more than the first—and most important—rank in the police service. Whatever their rank, all police officers serve 'in the office of constable'—in fact this is the title of one of England and Wales' most famous chief officers' autobiography.

WEBSITE

→ www.Policefederation.co.uk

FURTHER READING

Sir Robert Mark, *In The Office of Constable*, 1978, London: Harper Collins.

Walker, *Policing in a New Constitutional Order*, 2000, Sweet & Maxwell.

3

WHAT IT TAKES

In his recent report on police training (*Training Matters*, 2002), Her Majesty's Inspector of Constabulary, Robin Field-Smith said that:

In the future, the police service will be subjected to even closer scrutiny than today. Therefore, it is vital that it strives to ensure its people display the highest possible standards of attitudes and behaviour and are able to reflect, in their performance, every community's needs.

Not everyone is cut out to be a police officer or to undertake policing roles. The training is by no means easy and the job itself can be very demanding indeed. The recent 'Police Could You' advertising campaign gave a very impactive insight into some of the dilemmas and decisions that face police personnel. But what else does it take to carry out police duties effectively? A good starting point is competencies.

Competencies and standards

Police recruits will hear a lot about these. And if you've already been through the Recruit Assessment Centre, you will already have experienced a number of exercises that let you demonstrate your 'competencies'. Basically, competencies are the lists of skills, knowledge, attitudes and behaviours that are needed in order to be an efficient police officer. Different ranks and jobs in the police need different skills and knowledge and, for that reason, each role has its own list of competencies— whether it's the role of a police officer or a member of civilian support staff. The list of behaviours and attitudes that police officers will be expected to develop (with a lot of support and training of course) is set out below. Don't worry about the exact meaning or the detail—this list is included here so that you can become familiar with the things that officers will be trained in and measured against as they progress. You will already be good at some of these things. It's worth looking at the list and trying to spot those areas where you think you are strongest—and those where you are not. That will give you *your* view of yourself, and that's a good start; the views of your friends, family and partners may help you get a more accurate picture! During training, police officers are expected to assess their own levels of performance in these areas by getting the views of others and also to tell others how they are doing. As well as these general behaviours, there will be some further ones that are specific to the role you are given. The relevant activities that you will be expected (and trained) to carry out are also set out in other documents that you will be given.

Behaviours

Resilience

Shows reliability and resilience in difficult circumstances. Remains calm and confident, and responds logically and decisively in difficult situations.

Effective communication

Communicates all needs, instructions and decisions clearly. Adapts the style of communication to meet the needs of the audience. Asks probing questions to check understanding.

Community and customer focus

Provides a high level of service to customers. Maintains contact with customers, works out what they need and responds to them. Is aware of issues of diversity, and understands and is sensitive to cultural and racial differences.

Respect for diversity

Understands other people's views and takes them into account. Is tactful and diplomatic when dealing with people. Treats people with dignity and respect at all times, no matter what their background, status, circumstances or appearance.

Teamworking

Works effectively as a team member and helps build relationships within it. Actively helps and supports others to achieve team goals.

Personal responsibility

Takes personal responsibility for own actions and for sorting out issues or problems that arise. Is focused on achieving results to required standards and developing skills and knowledge.

Problem solving

Gathers enough relevant information to understand specific issues and events. Uses information to identify problems and draw logical conclusions. Makes good decisions.

Think about the things that you do in your everyday life and try to categorise them under the various headings above. You will see that you—and those around you—already do many of the things in the competency list. The police recruit assessment process aims to identify the most important competencies needed in the role, while initial training aims to develop those competencies, establishing new ones and building on the skills and abilities that you already have. The selection and training of other auxiliary and police staff works on the same basis.

Another key area in the development and performance of all police personnel is that of National Occupational Standards.

National Occupational Standards

How do you know whether someone is good at their job? If you were looking for a good plumber, surveyor or lawyer, how would you know whether they were competent? How do you define 'competent'? You would possibly start by looking at their qualifications, making sure that the person has gained the qualifications laid down in their particular industry. You might also look for membership of certain approved bodies such as the CORGI mark for gas installers—a bit like the kite mark for safety standards. But the bottom line is that you want to be confident that the person who is helping you has the skills and abilities necessary to carry out the job competently.

In a policing context you, as a member of the community, would want to know that any officer who came to help you was able to carry out the tasks of his or her role competently. Going back to our scenario of the visitor to London in the introduction to this book, the police officers there should be able to demonstrate the same level of competence no matter what particular police force they belong to. The only real way of ensuring this is by having a set of agreed occupational standards that all officers in all organisations are trained in and measured against.

Generally speaking, National Occupational Standards are ways of describing what competent performance looks like. They set out clearly, in plain language, what a person needs to achieve in carrying out a particular job or role. As 'national' standards, they apply to everyone in that particular job and don't vary from one part of the country (or countries) to another. National Occupational Standards are made up of several key parts, including:

- details of what the outcome is, e.g. completing and issuing a fixed penalty notice;
- what the person must be able to do to achieve this outcome, e.g. recognising the correct offences for issuing a fixed penalty notice, putting the correct detail, explaining the system to an offender;
- a range of different circumstances in which the person must be able to demonstrate competence, e.g. in a crowded street, in someone's house or at a police station;
- a way of assessing all the above reliably.

The police are introducing National Occupational Standards for all roles and ranks, including support and auxiliary staff. Responsibility for developing those standards has been given to the Police Skills and Standards Organisation (PSSO) and a number have already been introduced across England, Wales, Scotland and Northern Ireland.

These standards are used as a basis for police recruitment, development, training and promotion; they are also essential for managing a highly skilled workforce such as police personnel in general. Another major benefit of National Occupational Standards is that they tell you what your role is and what you have to do in order to carry it out competently. It may be that you have gained certain skills or qualifications in another job or role; there are ways of recognising these and making them count towards the standards required in the police (this is usually referred to as the accreditation of prior learning).

WEBSITE

→ www.psso.co.uk

FURTHER READING

Home Office Circular 42/2002.

4

WHO IT TAKES

Would I fit in?

A question asked by many people—especially younger ones—who are thinking about joining the police service or the 'police family' is whether they would 'fit in'. As you saw in the earlier chapters, policing deals with a wide variety of issues in the community—and it needs an equally wide variety of individuals to do it. Officers from all different social, cultural, religious and ethnic backgrounds train and work alongside each other.

Going back to the report by Her Majesty's Inspector of Constabulary (*Training Matters*, 2002) Robin Field-Smith said:

> Few other professions place so much importance on the way their members interact with customers and each other.

Every police force has a well-publicised equal opportunities policy which sets out the way in which individuals can expect to be treated. Of course the strict legal requirements which make it unlawful to discriminate against anyone as a result of their sex, race or married status in their employment apply just as much to the police as any other job. But forces' equal opportunities policies go further than that and usually guarantee your right to be treated equally regardless of rank, status or sexual orientation.

Joining the police

Joining the many thousand new probationary police officers and their tutors requires a lot of thought. The Home Office estimates that only 15% of applicants each year are successful. That shouldn't put you off—and, as you have seen in the last chapter, there are many other policing roles that can be done without signing up to be a police constable. But it should get you thinking very carefully about any career plans; it should also tell you what an achievement it is to succeed as a police officer.

In addition to the obvious areas of physical fitness and health, you will need to be emotionally strong and able to inspire confidence in those who will rely on you. You also need to be alert and observant. Can you remember (without looking!) what colour the face of your watch is and whether it has numbers, Roman numerals or just dots? Could you describe the person who sat next to you on the train, bus or Tube yesterday, or what your partner, parents or children were wearing when they left the house this morning? Some people are better at noticing the world around them than others—if you're going to be a police officer it's a habit worth getting into.

Minimum requirements

The minimum requirements as to physical fitness, ideal character profile and so on can be found in the Home Office application pack; they can also be accessed via the 'policecouldyou' website shown at the end of this chapter. There are various options for part-time and flexible working and the initial training for probationers is being reviewed in order to make it less rigid and more family-friendly. The requirements as to nationality have been removed and, in short, the routes open to people to join the police as constables have never been wider.

WEBSITE

→ www.policecouldyou.com

FURTHER READING

K. Thomas, C. Tolley and H. Tolley, *How to Pass the Police Initial Recruitment Test*, 2001, London: Kogan Page.

5

TRAINING AND DEVELOPMENT

'Training is fundamental to any organisation; ensuring that its people have the skills and knowledge effectively to do the jobs for which they were recruited should be paramount.' Her Majesty's Inspector of Constabulary (*Training Matters*, 2002, para. 7.19)

Training for police duty at every level is demanding. At the moment the exact training programme followed by a probationary police constable will depend on whether they join the Metropolitan Police service or one of the other police forces. Both initial training programmes have strong similarities and focus on developing knowledge, attitude, skills and behaviour needed for the modern policing role. You can find outlines for each programme at the back of this book. There are plans to standardise the whole system so that every police officer follows the same training programme; there are also plans to change some of the format that makes up the current programmes. If you do decide to join the police, you'll be told about any changes that might have happened.

Among the many advanced training opportunities available to potential recruits who are preparing for police duty are several new degree courses in policing. These are primarily available at the universities of Glamorgan in South Wales, Central England in Birmingham and Portsmouth. For further details, visit the websites shown at the end of this chapter.

Training style

Whether joining the Metropolitan Police or one of the other police forces, recruits and trainees will experience a variety of training styles. It's not a question of sitting in rows of desks learning the law and legal definitions. Although there is a fair amount of law to learn over the course of initial training—and indeed for the rest of your service—much of that can be studied outside the group training environment. Getting the law across is not necessarily the hardest bit of preparing for police duty. It's far harder to refine the power of persuasion than define the persuasion of power.

Although there will be some written assessments of your knowledge during initial training, there is a great emphasis on developing the relevant skills, understanding and behaviours as well. This means that the training styles take several forms including:

* research—individually and in groups
* presentation to others
* group discussion, led by an experienced trainer
* practical incidents, whereby you are given mock incidents to deal with in a safe and controlled environment
* distance and open learning, proceeding at your own pace through recommended materials—as you're doing now.

In addition to varied learning and training styles, there are many benefits to learning alongside other groups of people from different backgrounds. As a result, police training is increasingly being delivered in non-police environments such as local colleges and in conjunction with trainees from other jobs and walks of life.

Experiential learning

Much of police training is based around what is called 'experiential learning'. There's no great mystery about experiential learning—it's how most of us got this far in life already! Experiential learning is exactly what it says: learning from experience (either your own or someone else's)—and that includes mistakes. As a training method it means you get involved in relevant activities, at your own pace and under the guidance of an experienced trainer. But the key to the actual *learning* from an experience, however, comes from the period afterwards when you stop, look at what happened and reflect on how things went. This allows you to pick up the good points in the way in which you tackled a problem, consider what worked and what could have been done differently and to create a plan for future development—an Action Plan. The same process can be used when you watch others tackling issues and problems—you are able to learn from their experiences and plan to adopt or adapt parts of what you saw them do. If you've been involved in any form of sports training you'll probably be very familiar with the basic principles of experiential learning already. Also, if you've ever watched young children learning how to play computer games, you'll have seen its awesome power in action!

THE EXPERIENTIAL LEARNING CYCLE

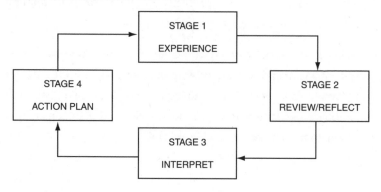

Experiential learning is usually an ongoing process, particularly if it involves things that you are likely to do over and over again in the future—like sporting manoeuvres, team tactics, job-related tasks (and computer games). For this reason, a lot of police training uses what is called the 'experiential learning cycle' (see previous page).

There are two important things to note about the model:

- It is a circular process with no clear beginning or end, representing learning as a continuous process—it's a *cycle*.

- As such, *all* stages have to be completed in the direction shown. Getting stuck at any stage is likely to hold up or frustrate any real learning.

You can see from the diagram that stage 1 is the experience itself. This might be an operational incident such as a domestic dispute or making an arrest, breath testing a motorist, issuing a fixed penalty notice; or it could be a training exercise. Stage 2 is the opportunity to review what happened and reflect, getting the views and feelings of others if appropriate. It's useful to make notes of thoughts, feelings, etc. at this stage, though it isn't always practical or appropriate to do so. This is one of the reasons that the Personal Development Profile (PDP) is so important. In a policing context, the PDP is central to making effective use of experiential learning. This document is looked at in more detail in Chapter 6. Stage 3 is the interpretation, that is, trying to make sense of what happened, why things worked out as they did and perhaps coming up with theories as to what might have happened if a different approach had been adopted.

Finally, there is stage 4, the Action Plan. This involves setting a plan for the future, deciding what to do and how to put it into practice. Action Planning is a critical part of an officer's development, not just as part of the experiential learning cycle, but also in setting objectives for performance appraisal and increasing professional competence. For this reason there is a further explanation of how to action plan and set development objectives below. You will note that the creation of the

Action Plan is itself an experience, leading you into the next cycle of learning.

Getting stuck

The possibility of getting stuck in the learning cycle was raised above. How and when can this happen? It can happen at any stage. Look at some examples:

Stage 1: experience

This is where many people get stuck in their everyday experiences that are nothing to do with work. People stuck at this stage don't seem to move on from their experiences—they simply have the same experience over and over again, making the same mistakes, ignoring the same advice or failing to consider the consequences of their earlier actions. People stuck here can generally be spotted by an 'I've always done it this way' attitude. Many poor drivers can be categorised under this heading: they may claim to have 20 years' experience of driving while, in reality, they've probably had the same few experiences which they've simply repeated every year for two decades.

Stage 2: review/reflect

If you're stuck here you are likely to be the type of person who logs what happened but never looks further than that. You may have lots of notes or diary entries but they're probably filed away somewhere, like new year's resolutions.

Stage 3: interpreting

Stuck here are your barrack room experts, the people who have been there, done it, got the proverbial 'T' shirt and will be happy to go back and do it all again next time in exactly the same way. People stuck at this stage have gained *some* learning from *some* experience. However, they've had all the experience they need thank you, and know how things should be done—according to them.

Experiential learning in practice

How does this look in a policing context? Once probationary police officers have completed the first stage of their initial training at a training centre, they work alongside an experienced police officer who will tutor them through real policing experiences. This tutor constable will help their new colleagues to prepare for certain incidents and calls, allowing them to take an appropriate level of responsibility at the scene and, most importantly, 'debriefing' the officer after the event. In this way, probationary police officers develop the knowledge, understanding, skills, attitudes and behaviours needed to police the community fairly and effectively. This then gives them the confidence and competence they need in order to become fitted for 'independent patrol'.

Look at an example of how this works:

EXAMPLE

A probationary police officer is working at a police station with her tutor constable. They are called to deal with a report of a traffic accident. The officer will have covered the basic rules and procedures in relation to traffic accidents while at a training centre. She will have learned the relevant law and what her powers are, and she may well have dealt with a mock 'accident' with her colleagues at the training centre, followed by a full review and interpretation of how well she had handled things—in line with the experiential learning cycle above.

Armed with this knowledge and experience, together with the support of the tutor constable, the probationary officer will go to the scene of the accident. She and her tutor constable will already have discussed

continued

continued

how much responsibility she is ready to take on and how confident she feels in dealing with certain situations. The tutor will allow the probationary officer to deal with those aspects of the accident scene that are appropriate—rendering first aid, taking details of witness, traffic control, or perhaps breathalysing the drivers (stage 1). After the incident has been resolved, both officers will take time out to review what happened and why (stage 2), how they dealt with the situation, what they might have done differently (stage 3) and what they will do next time in a similar situation (stage 4). In this way the probationary officer is able to learn from her own immediate experience and also from that of her tutor constable who is on hand to make sure that the job gets done properly.

Although the scenario described above is based around tutor constables and probationers, exactly the same principles apply in the training and development of Special Constables, Community Support Officers and any other operational police personnel.

Training by experience has proved far more effective than the 'inoculation method' whereby people have their dose and are thereby rendered immune from any further training treatment in that area. Listen to how many people say that they have 'had' their equal opportunities training or baton training or legal update training—as though it were some series of jabs needed before going on holiday. Unlike taking medicine, in training simply 'finishing the course' is not good enough.

WEBSITES

→ www.hmic.gov.uk
→ www.glam.ac.uk

→ www.uce.ac.uk
→ www.port.ac.uk

FURTHER READING

Training Matters, Report by Her Majesty's Inspector of Constabulary
(Training) HMSO, 2002.

6

FROM POTENTIAL TO PERFORMANCE

Another question asked by people joining the police is 'when does my training finish?' The answer is—it doesn't! Professional development must be a continuous process; as long as the world in which you work keeps changing and moving on, so must you.

One of the key features of police training—as you saw in the last chapter—is the concept of experiential learning. An essential part of that learning comes from recording what has taken place, what you did well and what you did that was not so good, what worked and what didn't, why, and what you could do next time when faced with similar circumstances.

One of the ways in which these questions are recorded is the Personal Development Profile (PDP). The idea of a PDP is that it allows you, your peers and supervisors to see how well you are performing, where your strengths lie in relation to the competencies required for your role and where (and how) you can develop those areas that need some work. The PDP is an invaluable tool that records not only what you've done during your initial training, but also how you have improved and where you can continue to develop in the future. In this sense the PDP is a bit like the navigation log used by pilots and sailors to chart their chosen courses—and to help you and others that might follow that route.

If you are going to chart future directions with any accuracy—and if you're going to check whether you made it or not—you will need a structured plan. In the context of police training and development, this means using action plans.

Action planning and objectives

One thing that a police officer has to get to grips with early in his or her training is the idea of action planning.

Action planning is not exclusive to the police and you may have come across it in some other field—in another job, as part of the Investors in People programme or something similar, through NVQ/SNVQs or even at college or school. It has become a regular feature of day-to-day management and self-development. Within the PDP system, and throughout his or her continuing professional development, police officers are expected to monitor their own individual progress against set targets and goals.

While there is no secret to action planning, there are several key features that are generally recognised as being essential to any effective Action Plan. These features are sometimes referred to by the acronym SMARTER.

S—Specific

If you are expected to demonstrate skills or behaviour, you will need to have a clear understanding of just what it is that is being asked of you. This means that any desired behaviour or competency must be specified at the start so that you know exactly what it is that is being measured.

Examples of specific objectives might be:

* to become competent in the use of a piece of equipment such as a roadside breathalyser

* to become familiar with the right forms that must be filled in such as fixed penalty notices

* to conduct an operational briefing of a group of people

* to attend and speak at a community forum.

This heading should deal with the 'what' part of the plan—what are you expected to do?

M—Measurable

If you are going to have anything approaching an accurate idea of how well you've achieved what you set out to do, you need to identify what you're trying to measure in the first place.

Useful measures of workplace performance are notoriously difficult to get right, particularly when subjective ideas such as attitude are introduced. How useful are objectives that say you should aim 'to get along with colleagues' or 'to communicate views appropriately'? Qualifying expressions such as *adequately* or *properly* will always be difficult to measure at the end of a performance review. It is probably more helpful to identify the relevant competency from your rank/role description and to select the relevant bits from it.

Measures of performance may be quantitative (e.g. 'how many', 'how much' or 'how often') or qualitative ('how well' or 'how efficiently'). The second type can be more attractive as they provide 'harder' data and are easier to evidence (e.g. 'how many fixed penalty notices did the person issue in a week?'). They also provide an easy comparison with previous performance or the performance of other people in the same job. However, such measures can be inappropriate, particularly where they relate to the use of discretionary powers by police officers (e.g. the number of people stopped and searched under the Police and Criminal Evidence Act 1984) as they can lead to 'league tables' whereby one person tries to outdo another.

Much police work is about evidence gathering and this heading should deal with the 'evidential' bit of your action plan—how will you and your trainers/tutors *know* whether you have developed or not?

A—Achievable

If an objective is not achievable it's not an 'objective'; it's a waste of time: yours and everybody else's.

Any meaningful Action Plan you set needs to contain objectives that you can achieve. This should be assessed in relation to:

* the time available
* your existing knowledge and skills
* the opportunities that will arise for you during the review period.

This heading should deal with the realistic nature of the plan—can these things be done by:

* you
* in this time frame
* with these opportunities/resources?

R—Relevant

Another practical consideration is the relevance of the objectives to:

* your overall performance and
* any areas raised at previous stages of the process.

If you are setting objectives, you should be able to look at the list and say that there are good reasons why you should achieve:

* these things
* in this way
* by this time.

This heading deals with the 'why' part of the plan—why are you aiming to do this? If you don't know, you need to start again.

T—Timely

Timing is important as a feature of an Action Plan in several respects. First, there must actually *be* some time limit identified and agreed at the outset. Secondly, the amount of time has an impact on the other headings set out above. If you haven't given yourself enough time or made it clear what timescales you are looking at, your plan will be unspecific, unmeasurable and/or unachievable.

Timing is also relevant to your Action Plan where a specific person is needed to assess and appraise your performance, either for continuity (e.g. where that person is only available for limited periods) or where they have a specific and relevant role in the process (e.g. a crime manager or a supervisor from a specialist department).

This heading should deal with the 'when' part of the plan—when are you expected to do these things and when will the process be reviewed/concluded?

E—Evaluated

The whole purpose of any Action Plan is to assess how far there has been any change in your relevant performance. You should evaluate your performance against the relevant parts of your Action Plan and within the agreed timescales.

This heading provides probably the most critical information, namely 'how far has your performance developed and improved towards the required standard?'

R—Recorded

Finally, every aspect of the action planning process must be accurately recorded. For probationary officers, this is done in the PDP system discussed above. After that, most forces operate a Continuing Professional Development (CPD) system containing all the relevant paperwork. All stages of the process should be documented and updated as necessary.

This heading addresses the 'where' part of the process—where is the relevant information to be found?

Professional conduct

You saw in Chapter 2 how holding the 'office of constable' and other policing roles means that a very high standard of behaviour is expected. You also saw the extract from the Code of Conduct which tells you and the community what those standards are in relation to police constables. The rest of that Code of Conduct is set out below. Have a look at it. Most of it is pretty obvious and amounts to little more than common sense. When you read it, think of the *opposite* behaviour and ask yourself how far you, your family and community would want that behaviour in the people trusted to police you.

1. Honesty and integrity
It is of paramount importance that the public has faith in the honesty and integrity of police officers. Officers should therefore be open and truthful in their dealings; avoid being improperly beholden to any person or institution; and discharge their duties with integrity.

2. Fairness and impartiality
Police officers have a particular responsibility to act with fairness and impartiality in all their dealings with the public and their colleagues.

3. Politeness and tolerance
Officers should treat members of the public and colleagues with courtesy and respect, avoiding abusive or deriding attitudes or behaviour. In particular, officers must avoid: favouritism of an individual or group; all forms of harassment, victimisation or unreasonable discrimination; and overbearing conduct to a colleague, particularly to one junior in rank or service.

4. Use of force and abuse of authority

Officers must never knowingly use more force than is reasonable, nor should they abuse their authority.

5. Performance of duties

Officers should be conscientious and diligent in the performance of their duties. Officers should attend work promptly when rostered for duty. If absent through sickness or injury, they should avoid activities likely to retard their return to duty.

6. Lawful orders

The police service is a disciplined body. Unless there is good and sufficient cause to do otherwise, officers must obey all lawful orders and abide by the provisions of Police Regulations. Officers should support their colleagues in the execution of their lawful duties, and oppose any improper behaviour, reporting it where appropriate.

7. Confidentiality

Information which comes into the possession of the police should be treated as confidential. It should not be used for personal benefit and nor should it be divulged to other parties except in the proper course of police duty. Similarly, officers should respect, as confidential, information about force policy and operations unless authorised to disclose it in the course of their duties.

8. Criminal offences

Officers must report any proceedings for a criminal offence taken against them. Conviction of a criminal offence may of itself result in further action being taken.

9. Property

Officers must exercise reasonable care to prevent loss or damage to property (excluding their own personal property but including police property).

10. Sobriety

Whilst on duty officers must be sober. Officers should not consume alcohol when on duty unless specifically authorised to do so or it becomes necessary for the proper discharge of police duty.

11. Appearance

Unless on duties which dictate otherwise, officers should always be well turned out, clean and tidy whilst on duty in uniform or in plain clothes.

12. General conduct

Whether on or off duty, police officers should not behave in a way which is likely to bring discredit upon the police service.

It is worth noting that, as well as setting out the duties that police officers have towards members of the community, the Code also includes their *duties to each other*. This reinforces what was said in Chapter 4 by the HMIC Robin Field-Smith and is worth remembering if you are still undecided about joining the police and are concerned about how you might be treated by some colleagues.

Another point worth noting is that some parts of the Code apply whether a police officer is on or off duty. However, where off duty behaviour is concerned, this will be measured against the generally accepted standards of the day. This takes us back to the point at the very start of the book—that police officers are simply citizens in uniform.

If police officers breach the Code they can face disciplinary proceedings and, in serious cases, dismissal from the service; similar sanctions exist for auxiliary staff. There are also separate rules for monitoring poor performance of police officers. This is different from the Code of Conduct and involves a number of meetings and interviews that will be put in place if someone is *persistently* performing poorly. Although this procedure can also lead to dismissal in some extreme cases, it is meant to let officers know in which areas they are not getting things right and give them the chance to improve.

Probationer constables

During their probationary period, constables are also subject to two important parts of the 1995 Police Regulations: regulations 14 and 15.

Regulation 14 allows a chief officer to extend the probationary period of a constable; regulation 15 allows the chief officer to dispense with the officer's services if that chief officer considers that the constable is not likely to be mentally or physically fitted to performing their duties, or that he or she is unlikely to become an efficient or 'well conducted' officer. In other words, the probationary period is truly that: you have plenty of chances to succeed—and the support to do so—but, if necessary, your probationary period can be extended or ultimately terminated by the relevant chief officer.

WEBSITES

→ www.policecouldyou.co.uk
→ www.homeoffice.gov.uk

FURTHER READING

Fraser Sampson and Niran De Silva (John Bowers ed.), *Police Conduct, Complaints and Efficiency*, 2001, Oxford: Blackstone Press (OUP).
Ainsworth, *Psychology and Policing*, 2002, William Publishing.

PART II

POLICING POWERS

7

HUMAN RIGHTS AND POLICE POWERS

Many countries have a written constitution—that is, a very formal legal declaration of what rights and freedoms its citizens are entitled to. A good example is the United States. England and Wales has no written constitution as such; the closest thing is the European Convention on Human Rights, most of which was made a specific part of our domestic law by the Human Rights Act 1998. You may have heard a great deal about this Act and the European Convention in the media—before and since the Act came into force.

The European Convention on Human Rights

Its full name is 'The European Convention for the Protection of Human Rights and Fundamental Freedoms'. It is a Treaty between governments and is by no means 'new'. It was signed in 1959 by the governments of those countries making up the Council of Europe and was intended to give full legal protection to the most fundamental rights and freedoms necessary in democratic societies. In looking at the Convention, it is important to remember the background of events that led up to it. At the time the Convention was drawn up, many European countries were still trying to come to terms with the lessons of the Second World War and it is against the backdrop of a war-ravaged Europe and an emerging Soviet Union that the Convention was written. This history lesson is useful because it explains some of the wording used within the Convention, wording that may sound a bit out of place within the modern democratic setting of England and Wales.

Since then, the Convention has been adopted by a majority of countries throughout Europe—including some former communist States—and has been used as a blueprint by a great many others.

Human Rights Act 1998

The 1998 Act is a very significant piece of legislation—particularly for police officers. Not only does it give effect to the fundamental rights contained within the European Convention (see below), the Act also affects the way in which all other legislation must be interpreted and applied. Wherever possible, all laws and legal proceedings in England and Wales—criminal and civil—must be applied in a way that is compatible with people's Convention rights.

Public authorities

A very important feature of the European Convention is that is aimed at creating rights against the State and public authorities—and so is the 1998 Act. Although it creates new remedies against 'public authorities', the Act does not create any new rights in private matters between individuals. Just because someone next to you on the Tube infringes your right to a private life by playing dance music on their stereo, does not mean that you can take them to court. You might have some other legal arguments available to you but the Human Rights Act 1998 is not one of them.

So the important thing to look for when considering the Human Rights Act 1998 is a 'public authority'. Whether something is a 'public authority' or not will usually be decided by looking at the type of work or function that the organisation carries out. Some public authorities are pretty obvious, e.g. courts and tribunals, police, fire and ambulance services and local authorities. These organisations, and the people working for them, have a duty to pay due regard to the Convention rights of individuals when exercising *any and all* of their functions. Other organisations that might fall into this category (and therefore have to take note of the Act) include security companies running prisons/ prisoner escort services at police stations, public transport operators and other public bodies such as the BBC.

As you read through the next few chapters, you will come across boxes in the text. You'll have seen similar ones in the earlier chapters. These boxes are designed to reinforce the relevant points and to stretch your understanding; they're also supposed to keep it interesting. Here's an example:

ATTENTION TO DETAIL

Did you notice at this point that you might be able to use the European Convention to deal with the 'passenger with the noisy stereo' (above), not by using it against the passenger himself but against the *Tube operators* because they might be a 'public authority'?

What are the 'Convention rights'?

The rights and freedoms protected by the European Convention are pretty much what you would expect. Think about the things which make up a true democracy, the basic rights and freedoms that you would want for you and your family, your friends and neighbours. What rights and freedoms would you include in the list? Most, if not all, of those things are covered in the Convention. In fact, some of them are so fundamental that they are often taken for granted in many countries—like the right to life and freedom of speech.

You won't have to learn the Convention Articles and Protocols but you do need to know generally what they say. The Convention rights are as follows. Don't worry about the Article or Protocol numbers; it's the principles that matter:

Right to life (Article 2)

Everyone's right to life shall be protected by law.

Freedom from torture (Article 3)

No one shall be subjected to torture or to inhuman or degrading treatment or punishment.

Freedom from slavery and forced labour (Article 4)

No one shall be held in slavery or servitude.
No one shall be required to perform forced or compulsory labour.

Right to liberty and security (Article 5)

Everyone has the right to liberty and security of person. No one shall be deprived of his/her liberty save in accordance with a procedure prescribed by law.

Everyone who is arrested shall be informed promptly, in a language which he/she understands, of the reasons for his/her arrest and of any charge against him/her.

Everyone arrested or detained shall be brought promptly before a judge or other officer and shall be entitled to trial within a reasonable time or to release pending trial.

Right to a fair trial (Article 6)

In the determination of his/her civil rights and obligations or of any criminal charge against him/her, everyone is entitled to a fair and public hearing within a reasonable time by an independent and impartial tribunal established by law.

Everyone charged with a criminal offence shall be presumed innocent until proved guilty.

No punishment without crime (Article 7)

No one shall be held guilty of any criminal offence on account of any act or omission which did not constitute a criminal offence under national or international law at the time when it was committed.

Right to private life (Article 8)

Everyone has the right to respect for his/her private and family life, home and correspondence.

Freedom of thought (Article 9)

Everyone has the right to freedom of thought, conscience and religion.

Freedom of expression (Article 10)

Everyone has the right to freedom of expression.

Freedom of assembly and association (Article 11)

Everyone has the right to freedom of peaceful assembly and to freedom of association with others, including the right to form and to join trade unions for the protection of his/her interests.

Right to marry (Article 12)

Men and women of marriageable age have the right to marry and to found a family, according to the national laws of that State.

Prohibition of discrimination in Convention rights (Article 14)

The enjoyment of the rights and freedoms set forth in this Convention shall be secured without discrimination on any ground such as sex, race, colour, language, religion, political or other opinion, national or social origin, association with a national minority, property, birth or other status.

Protection of property (Protocol 1)

Every natural or legal person is entitled to the peaceful enjoyment of his/her possessions.

Right to education (Protocol 1)

No person shall be denied the right to education.

Right to free elections (Protocol 1)

The parties undertake to hold free elections at reasonable intervals by secret ballot, under conditions which will ensure the free expression of the opinion of the people.

There should be no real surprises here—these Convention rights and freedoms are no more and no less than you have probably come to expect living in England and Wales.

If you are looking for Article 13, it is not specifically included by the 1998 Act, but its terms—the right to effective remedies where your other rights are breached—are covered in other rules and procedures.

Although everyone is entitled to some protection so far as those rights are concerned, there are several practical considerations to bear in mind. The first is the fact that some of the rights and freedoms are more important or fundamental than others. Secondly, the exercise of one person's individual rights might well impact on the rights and freedoms of others; it might also be in direct conflict with another person's individual right. These practical issues, which are of great importance to the police, are discussed below.

```
            GUMBERG LIBRARY
          DUQUESNE UNIVERSITY
            (412) 396-6130

patron's name:Conti, Norman

  title:Blackstone's preparing fo
  author:Sampson, Fraser.
 item id:35282005802122
    due:6/13/2006,23:59

  title:Upgrading the American po
  author:Saunders, Charles B.
 item id:35282003146845
    due:6/13/2006,23:59

  title:The quality of police edu
  author:Sherman, Lawrence W.
 item id:35282000532435
    due:6/13/2006,23:59

     http://www.library.duq.edu
       REFERENCE - 412.396.6133
       CIRCULATION - 412.396.6130
National Library Week April 10-16
```

Balancing competing rights and needs

Some of the European Convention's provisions are described as being *absolute*. That means there is no room for debate, no watering down of their protection; infringement of them is prohibited—full stop. The right to freedom from torture (under Article 3) is an example. However, some other rights are limited or restricted in some way, such as the right to liberty under Article 5. These rights couldn't be absolute if you think about it. If, say, the right to freedom of movement were 'absolute', that would allow no restriction of the right whatsoever. Therefore there could be no arrest or imprisonment of anyone— whatever they had done wrong. So you can see that these other rights have to be restricted if the 'democratic society' is going to work. If a person is lawfully arrested or detained, his or her right to liberty has been infringed, but the Convention takes account of such situations. Similarly, there will be times when the freedom of an individual conflicts with the general public interest—the right to freedom of assembly against the need to maintain public order for instance. These categories of rights are generally referred to as 'qualified' rights and the areas of potential conflict they raise are of particular significance to the police. *Very often, the job of the police is to help balance the rights of an individual with those of society as a whole.* There are some places where the inhabitants enjoy unrestricted freedom to make noise, charge around taking each others' things, invading each others' space and say whatever they want—they are toddlers' play areas and anyone who has tried refereeing one of those for anything more than a minute will understand what anarchy really looks like! Just as a person's rights need to be balanced against those of the community generally, so too must they be balanced where they directly compete with one another. An example would be a celebrity's right to respect for their private life when they hold a glitzy wedding and a glossy magazine's freedom of expression when they want to publish photographs of that wedding. Go through the list again and you will be able to think of many more. Indeed, the potential for such rights to conflict, particularly in the areas of neighbour disputes, is painfully clear to most police officers.

The important job for the police, the courts, local authorities and others is to *balance* these rights against each other and against the needs of the democratic society within which they exist. For this reason many of the Convention's Articles include any relevant limitations or exceptions. Although each is different, there are three key features that need to be considered in achieving this balance—the 'three tests'.

The three tests

Where the European Convention gives individuals a particular right, any limitation will be carefully examined and cautiously applied. Otherwise, it could be trumped or overridden by any number of 'get out' clauses. Therefore, in very general terms, any limitations on a Convention right must be:

* prescribed by law
* intended to achieve a legitimate objective
* necessary and proportionate.

Let's look at these a bit more closely.

Test 1: prescribed by law

This means that there must be some clearly published law allowing the restriction on someone's Convention rights. Acts of Parliament that give the police powers (see below) are good examples of something meeting this first test. However, one of the ways in which oppressive States have got around the individual rights of their citizens in the past is by simply passing laws that allow them to do so—however unpleasant, unfair or unacceptable that law might be. The Human Rights Act 1998, says that a government minister must sign off any new laws before they are made, certifying that they are compatible with people's Convention rights. But this still does not control the way in which those laws and powers might be *used*; hence the reason for test 2.

Test 2: intended to achieve a legitimate objective

This prevents the use of powers that are prescribed by law (as above) being used for the wrong purpose or wrong reasons. This second test makes sure that, just because the police, courts and other public author-ities have got legal powers (say, to arrest people and search their prop-erty), they do not use them improperly. However, that is still not enough to safeguard individual rights and freedoms. A further safety net is needed—test 3.

Test 3: necessary and proportionate

Any actions by public authorities that interfere with someone's Convention rights must be 'necessary and proportionate to the end that is to be achieved'. Even though you might have a legal power contained in an Act of Parliament (passing test 1) and you use it to achieve a legitimate objective (passing test 2), your behaviour might be com-pletely over the top and heavy handed. Test 3 means that you can only use that power if you can show that it was necessary to do so. Put another way, it means that public authorities cannot 'use a sledgehammer to crack a nut' (as the saying goes).

ATTENTION TO DETAIL

Your car is seen speeding by a speed camera on a motorway. In these circumstances the police have powers to ask you who was driving the car at the time. They also have other general powers to enter people's property and to carry firearms. Although these police powers come from Acts of Parliament (meeting test 1) and catching speeding motorists is a legitimate objective (test 2), that does not mean that the police can send a firearms team crashing through the windows of your home just because your car was caught by a speed camera and they want to know who was driving it!

The important things to remember when dealing with issues of human rights law are:

* Is there a 'public authority' involved? Don't forget that the courts are public authorities so, even in purely private disputes such as sales of goods, any relevant Convention rights will need to be considered. Police officers, Special Constables and auxiliaries such as Community Support Officers are also public authorities.

* Most Convention rights can be limited in some way—check the wording of the Article itself.

* If there is any interference with a Convention right, apply the three tests to see how the courts may look at the situation.

* Note that this area of law does not exist on its own—it touches on every other aspect of law, whether that be police powers, the laws of evidence or the wording of criminal offences themselves.

As you study each area of police law and procedure, keep these principles in mind—it's surprising where they can crop up.

WEBSITE

→ www.blackstonespolicemanuals.com

8

POWERS OF ARREST

As you saw in Chapter 1, police officers and their colleagues are entrusted with many powers and privileges. The most important of these powers, both practically and constitutionally, are the powers of arrest, search, entry and seizure. You have probably heard TV cops talking about getting warrants to arrest suspects, and news programmes refer to this process all the time. However, police powers of arrest in England and Wales are pretty extensive and it is quite rare for an arrest warrant to be needed. But this is an important point: all of the main police powers can be separated into those which *do* need to be authorised first by a warrant from the courts and those which can be executed by the officer himself/herself without having to ask the court for authority.

Wherever policing powers come from, it is essential that police officers and others use them wisely, fairly and properly. In addition to the human rights aspects discussed in Chapter 7, using powers improperly can lead to officers being liable, both in civil and criminal law and under the Code of Conduct (see Chapter 6); it can also lead to evidence being excluded and criminals being allowed to go free. But, perhaps most importantly, the way in which they use their powers has a direct effect on the confidence that the community has in its police. Even where police powers are exercised *lawfully*, how, when and where they are used by individual officers can be *perceived* as a source of oppression and discrimination, leading to a reduction in confidence in the police and the creation of an atmosphere of distrust. The risks of police powers being perceived in this way were highlighted very clearly in the Report into the murder of Stephen Lawrence in 1999.

At this point it would be useful to go back to the discussion about using *discretion* in Chapter 2.

If you ask anyone what special powers the police have that other citizens do not, they will probably come up with powers of arrest first. Powers of arrest generally are therefore probably the most widely-known policing powers—and the most widely misunderstood. Once you have looked closely at them you will see that there are many situations where anyone has powers to arrest the offender, not just the police. There are, however, some very important areas where the police are entrusted with specific powers to arrest and detain suspects.

So what is an 'arrest'? If you had to guess, you'd probably say that it was taking someone to a police station against their will and that wouldn't be a bad summary. An arrest generally involves stopping someone from going where they please—there's no need to take them anywhere—but arrests will usually be made in connection with an allegation over something that has already taken place such as the offences discussed in later chapters. The taking of someone's liberty to answer an allegation probably distinguishes arrests from *detention*. The police have powers to detain people for reasons other than answering an alleged charge—an example would be under the Football (Disorder) Act 2000 which allows people who have been banned from attending matches to be detained to stop them travelling to a game. Similarly, there are some auxiliary police staff such as Community Support Officers who are given powers to detain people under certain circumstances until the arrival of a police officer. These powers are best treated as being separate from traditional arrests made by the police.

Although arrests in this sense are usually made in connection with an offence that has taken place, occasionally arrests may be made for other things such as:

- to *prevent* something taking place (such as where a person is arrested in connection with a 'breach of the peace' discussed in Chapter 12)
- to take DNA samples or fingerprints
- to return someone to prison or bring them before a court.

Usually a person will be arrested because the police officer suspects that they have done something wrong. However, there are also occasions where a person can be arrested because they:

- are *about* to do something wrong
- might do something wrong if they're not arrested
- have *not done* something—e.g. failed to blow into a breathalyser when required to do so.

It is important to note (that's why the next bit is in italics) that *the police are not under any general duty to arrest and should always consider the use of other methods where appropriate.*

ATTENTION TO DETAIL

You will see from the description that an arrest is also an interference with a person's European Convention rights (to liberty and freedom of movement). Therefore the three tests will apply to the use of any powers of arrest by the police or other public authorities.

Lawful arrests

Every arrest must be lawful—otherwise it is *unlawful*. This startlingly obvious piece of wisdom is an important thing to remember. The person carrying out any arrest—like *anyone* using *any* legal power—must be able to point to some legal authority which allows them to do it; otherwise their actions will be unlawful. This rule overlaps with test 1 under the human rights provisions in Chapter 7. Legal authority for a power of arrest may come from the following sources:

• the nature of the offence
• the circumstances at the time
• the provisions of a particular Act
• an order (e.g. a court order or a warrant).

The last of these is in italics because you should note it for now and then forget about it—at least for a while. Powers that come from warrants or orders are pretty easy—the court tells you to do something and you do it. The main police powers that will concern you, however, are set out in various Acts of Parliament and are the powers discussed earlier in this chapter. Police officers are allowed to use these powers without any further permission or authority. These are described as powers *without warrant*.

Many (but not all) police powers of arrest, search, entry and seizure come from one particular Act—the Police and Criminal Evidence Act 1984. This is generally referred to as 'PACE' and, like most Acts of Parliament, even though it was passed some time ago, it is regularly amended and updated. What follows below relates to powers of arrest *without warrant*.

Arrestable offences

Let's start by getting rid of a myth. The police cannot just arrest anyone for anything. In some ways it might be better if they could as it would reduce their training to several weeks; it would also lead to a 'police state' which would undermine one of the main features of a democratic society. So, unfortunately for those studying the subject (but fortunately for everyone else), the situation is far more complicated. Although they have wide powers of arrest, police officers cannot arrest anyone just because they think that person has committed an offence. Some criminal offences carry their own power of arrest, others depend on the circumstances surrounding the offence or the offender. Although this area is quite complex, there is a key feature that you should grasp very early on. This is the concept of the 'arrestable offence'.

What is an 'arrestable offence'? Common sense would tell you that it is any criminal offence for which you can be arrested. If only life were that simple! Unfortunately, in many areas common sense and the law are often total strangers—and this bit is no exception. The expression 'arrestable offence' has a very particular meaning and you might as well get to grips with that meaning right from the start.

You will find the definition of an 'arrestable offence' in PACE (section 24 and schedule 1A if you're interested). This says that arrestable offences are offences:

- for which the sentence is fixed by law (and there's only one such offence—murder)
- for which a person (not previously convicted) can be sentenced to five years' imprisonment or more
- all the other offences listed in Schedule 1A.

Taking the first two above, you can see that these form the most serious criminal offences. Murder, manslaughter, rape, robbery, theft, burglary, assaults, criminal damage—all the offences that you will have heard of in the news and elsewhere are all 'arrestable offences' (these offences are set out in greater detail in Chapter 12). But remember *this does not mean that these are the only offences for which people can be arrested.*

The last one is a bit more complicated. Schedule 1A sets out a list of other offences that are 'arrestable offences' because Parliament says they are. As well as being serious offences, they also contain offences that are of concern within the community at the moment. These are offences such as carrying knives and other weapons, offences involving racial hatred, harassment and football disorder, having indecent photographs of children and taking vehicles without the owners' consent.

So what?

Does it matter if some offences are called 'arrestable' offences? The answer is 'yes'. This is important because there are several distinctions between arrestable offences and other types of offence. First, the powers of arrest without warrant for arrestable offences are much more straightforward. These are explained below. Another distinction is that other wide powers (e.g. to enter premises) are available if the offence you are dealing with is an 'arrestable' offence.

Arresting for an arrestable offence

Briefly, anyone can arrest someone who:

* is in the act of committing an arrestable offence
* he or she has reasonable grounds for *suspecting to be committing* an arrestable offence, or
* (where an arrestable offence has been committed) is guilty of committing it.

This means that, in relation to most significant offences, every citizen may have a power of arrest. You have probably heard of people making a 'citizen's arrest' and this is where the powers would usually come from. What the average citizen does not have, however, is the training to help them decide when it is appropriate to use a power of arrest; nor do they have the practical experience and professional competence to carry out the arrest properly, safely and confidently.

Police officers and police staff have these 'citizen's' powers but also have some wider powers of arrest in relation to arrestable offences. For instance, police officers may arrest someone where they have reasonable grounds to suspect that an arrestable offence has been committed; they can also arrest someone whom they suspect is *about to* commit an arrestable offence.

Occasionally, some other people not employed by the police are given the powers and privileges of a constable. Examples are some prison officers within their prisons and employees of the Independent Police Complaints Commission.

These areas are covered in far more detail in officers' initial training. The important thing at this stage is that you know that some offences are classed as being 'arrestable' and carry wide powers of arrest. The police may have some other power of arrest for other offences which are not classed as 'arrestable' but the two are very different things.

Non-arrestable offences

So what happens where the offence is *not* an 'arrestable offence'? Apart from a few exceptions, the answer is where you will have guessed it to be by now—in PACE.

Where a police officer has reasonable grounds for suspecting that any non-arrestable offence has been committed, he or she may arrest the relevant person under certain conditions. Those conditions include occasions where there is no other way of dealing with the offence because the person won't give their name and address or where an arrest is necessary to prevent someone getting injured.

Does this mean that the police have powers to arrest for offences that are not 'arrestable'? Yes. Don't worry if that's confusing—it confused a number of members of the House of Commons recently in passing the Police Reform Act. Although the idea of being able to arrest someone for an offence that is not an arrestable offence may sound daft, it's only confusing if you don't understand the meaning of 'arrestable offence'. That's why it is vital to understand that 'arrestable offences' and 'offences for which you can be arrested' are not the same thing.

ATTENTION TO DETAIL

Arrestable offences and offences for which you can be arrested are not the same thing.

It's worth saying twice.

So why aren't all offences arrestable? This is a good question, but one that is not answered here. The real point is that, if there wasn't a general power of arrest for all offences, police officers would have some considerable practical problems. For instance, as a police officer you might stop a driver who had no driving licence (a non-arrestable offence) and require his details in order to report him for the offence. The driver could simply give his name as Mickey Mouse and then drive away. Likewise, you could be called to a public play area in a park where a group of people had been throwing beer cans and cigarette ends around, upsetting children and parents (another non-arrestable offence). If the group refused to give their names and addresses and said that they were going to come back and make things worse after you'd gone, there would not be much that you could do about it.

While it's true that just having a power available doesn't mean that you have to use it, it's necessary for the police to have some general arrest power to use where there is no arrestable offence involved. Let's take a closer look at this very useful power of arrest.

Arresting for non-arrestable offences

There are three main elements to the general power of arrest (which you'll find under section 25 of PACE).

When

The first element deals with *when* the power of arrest might be available. This is when there are:

* reasonable grounds for suspecting
* that *any* offence—other than an 'arrestable offence'—however minor
* *has been* committed/attempted, or
* *is being* committed/attempted.

Who

The second element deals with *who* can be arrested using this power. This is *any* person who the officer has reasonable grounds to suspect of:

* having committed/attempted to commit the offence, or
* being in the course of committing/attempting to commit the offence.

Why

The third element deals with *why* that person should be arrested. This is generally because it appears to the officer that using a summons to deal with person is not practical or is inappropriate because any of the general arrest conditions are satisfied.

It is therefore generally assumed that other procedures (such as reporting the person for summons or issuing a fixed penalty notice) will be the first choice when dealing with the relevant person and it is only if a 'general arrest condition' applies that a person can be arrested under this power.

General arrest conditions

The general arrest conditions are:

* that the person's name is not known and cannot be readily ascertained
* that the officer has reasonable grounds for doubting the name or address given, or
* that the officer has reasonable grounds for believing that arrest is necessary to prevent the person—
  * causing or suffering physical injury
  * causing loss or damage to property
  * committing an offence against public decency or
  * causing an unlawful obstruction of the highway
* that the constable has reasonable grounds for believing that arrest is necessary to protect a child or other vulnerable person from the person.

It is important to note that it's not generally *an offence* for a person to refuse to give their name and address to the police and that here it's a condition that can trigger the general power of arrest. There are times where it *is* an offence to give a false name and address to a police officer or to give no name at all (but this isn't one of them). The times where it is an offence in itself to give false details or none at all are usually road traffic cases or cases where the person is suspected of anti-social behaviour. These are completely separate from the general arrest conditions.

ATTENTION TO DETAIL

You may wonder what happens if, having had the chance to re-think the wisdom of using Mickey Mouse's name, the relevant person decides to give their real name and address on the way to the police station?

If the grounds for detaining the arrested person come to an end before they reach a police station and there are no further grounds for detaining them, the officer must release the person.

Tell them what's happening

Whether an arrest is made for an arrestable offence or for any other offence, the law (PACE) makes it very clear that the person *must* be told that he or she is under arrest and why—even if it should be obvious to them.

The only exception here is where the person has escaped before the officer could give him or her the relevant information. Even if the person is being violent or aggressive, they must be told that they are being arrested and given the reason for it as soon as practicable.

ATTENTION TO DETAIL

These requirements come from the Police and Criminal Evidence Act 1984 (PACE). However, remember that Article 5 of the European Convention on Human Rights says that:

Everyone who is arrested shall be informed promptly, in a language

continued

continued

which he/she understands, of the reasons for his/her arrest and of any charge against him/her.

Therefore, there is an added requirement to make sure that arrested person is given the information in a language they understand. This is particularly important where you are dealing with someone whose first language is not English.

The other thing that you have to remember to tell people when they are arrested—or indeed questioned about an offence—is the caution.

A word of caution

One of the first things that you will need to learn if training to be a police officer or investigator is the 'caution'. Anyone who has seen American cop movies will be familiar with the caution—or at least the idea behind it. Think of the part where the arresting officer begins 'You have the right to remain silent. You have the right to an attorney' etc. Well, with some minor differences, this is very similar to the caution.

ATTENTION TO DETAIL

The more compulsive movie addicts will know that the process in the United States is called the *Miranda* process. This comes from the case where the US Supreme Court decided that all suspects must be read their rights when arrested (*Miranda v The State of Arizona*). By this stage you should be able to guess where the English and Welsh equivalent comes from—PACE.

Before you get to the exact wording of the caution, you should note that it is the *principle* behind it that is the most important part. It is designed to alert the person who is being arrested of their right not to say anything and that anything they say may be used against them in court later. It is also a warning that *by not saying anything* they may be harming any defence which they later use in court.

The actual *wording* of the caution is designed to get this message across in the easiest way and it has been carefully written. Although some minor variations in the wording are allowed by the courts, if you get the words wrong, you may well get the message wrong and this would be unfair to the person under arrest. This is why (going back to the movies for a minute) you see the law enforcement characters in American films reading the words from a card—literally *reading* the suspect their rights so there can be no argument later as to the exact words that the officer used.

The wording for the caution is therefore important and police officers will know it by heart before they complete their initial training (it also comes up in the occasional pub quiz). You will find it in the Codes of Practice at the back of PACE (Code C, para. 10.4). It goes like this:

> *You do not have to say anything. But it may harm your defence if you do not mention when questioned something which you later rely on in court. Anything you do say may be given in evidence.*

Thirty-seven words which you should really start to learn now.

Generally speaking, PACE requires that a person must be cautioned when they are arrested (they should also be cautioned before being questioned about their suspected involvement in any criminal offence).

ATTENTION TO DETAIL

It should be no surprise that not everyone agrees to 'come quietly' when they are arrested. You may wonder then what happens when the officer is not able to get through these 37 words when wrestling with a violent drunk. Thankfully, here the law and common sense coincide. PACE says that you do not have to administer the caution where the behaviour or the condition of the person arrested makes it impracticable to do so. This is slightly different from the requirement to tell people that they are being arrested and why (see above).

The Code goes on to provide that, if a person does not appear to understand what the caution means, the officer who has given it should go on to explain it in his or her own words. This is not only important when dealing with people whose first language is other than English but also where there is some doubt about the person's ability to understand what is happening generally. If in doubt, err on the side of 'caution'!

A word about force

The Police and Criminal Evidence Act 1984 allows the use of *reasonable force* when making an arrest. Other Acts also allow the use of such force as is reasonably necessary in the arrest of people and the prevention of crime. Whether any force used is 'reasonable' will be decided by the court in the light of all the circumstances, including the situation as the arresting officer believed it to be at the time. On some very extreme and rare occasions, the force used by a police officer may even be lethal to the other person. Police officers are given expert training in the proper ways to respond to situations where any force is anticipated.

FURTHER READING

Report of the Inquiry into the murder of Stephen Lawrence, 1999, London: HMSO.

9

STOP AND SEARCH

In addition to their special powers of arrest, another important power given to the police is the power to stop and search people and vehicles. This is probably one of the most controversial police powers and it's vital that officers have a full understanding, not only of what the powers are, but how and when they should be used.

By this point there is probably no need to say where the power comes from—it's found in the Police and Criminal Evidence Act 1984 (PACE)—right at the beginning in fact. PACE also has some Codes of Practice to help people interpret its provisions and set guidelines to be followed. These Codes must be made available in police stations. The relevant Code of Practice setting out how stop and search powers should be used are in Code A.

Where?

Generally, a police officer may use the power to stop and search in public places. This will include places that are open to the public on payment (such as museums, railway stations, cinemas, etc.). It does not include people's homes. However, if the person to be searched is in a garden which is part of a house, the power to search can be used if the officer has 'reasonable grounds for believing' that the person doesn't live there *and* that they are not there with the permission of someone who does. This makes sense. While people don't want to be routinely searched in their own gardens, it is necessary that the police have a power to search people who are found in *someone else's* garden—as burglars often are! This is a good example of the 'balancing' act that the police and Parliament need to do in terms of people's competing human rights.

These restrictions don't mean that the search itself has to be carried out in the place where the person was stopped; they are restrictions on where the person you want to search must have been found. In fact, for some searches, the person should be taken away from public view. This might be seen by the person stopped as a bit sinister but it's intended to save them from embarrassment.

What?

The officer may search any person, any vehicle and anything that is in or on the vehicle (such as luggage, roofboxes, etc.). The officer may search the person or vehicle for stolen or prohibited articles. These are generally weapons or tools for use in burglaries, etc.

ATTENTION TO DETAIL

Now that you know about arrests and the fact that even the police can't detain people without a specific lawful power to do so, you should be asking how PACE searches can be carried out without a further power to stop the person from just walking away. The answer is they can't. That's why the power to stop and search also includes a power to detain the person and their vehicle for the purpose of searching them. As you'd expect, you can only detain someone for such time as is reasonably necessary for the search to be carried out.

When?

Before he or she can use the power to stop and search, an officer must have 'reasonable grounds for suspecting' that he or she will find stolen or prohibited articles. Whether as the police officer you would have such reasonable grounds must decided in light of all the circumstances at the time. Usually it will be the behaviour of the person concerned or information that someone else has given which will help you decide whether there are such 'reasonable grounds' to suspect you'll find the stolen or prohibited articles. But you must actually *have* a such a reasonable suspicion. If, in fact, you know that there is little or no likelihood of finding the articles (perhaps because you saw the person throw them into a canal or give them to someone else), the power cannot be used.

Reasonable suspicion can never be founded on the basis of purely personal factors such as a person's colour, age or hairstyle. The dangers of stereotyping people on their appearance or perceived membership of a particular group are discussed in Chapter 13. However, as well as being a matter of common respect for diversity, the fact that police officers must not stop and search people on the basis of personal features alone is also made quite clear in PACE—Code A of the Codes of Practice.

Nevertheless, Code A does make provision for the searching of members of gangs or groups who habitually carry:

* knives unlawfully or
* weapons or
* controlled drugs

and wear distinctive items of clothing or other things to identify themselves with such a gang or group.

How?

This is very important. Code A sets out *how* any search must be carried out. The co-operation of the person must be sought in every case and, although force could ultimately be used, this should be viewed very much as a last resort and used only where the person has shown that they are unwilling to co-operate or where they resist.

If, in the course of a search, the officer does find a stolen or prohibited article, he or she may seize it. Also, of course, if there are any grounds to suspect that the person has committed any offence, they should be cautioned (in the way described earlier) before any questions are put to them.

ATTENTION TO DETAIL

One oddity about the power under PACE is that it doesn't authorise the officer to stop a vehicle. This power generally comes from the Road Traffic Act 1988 and the officer must be wearing uniform at the time.

Having stopped a person to search them, there is no *requirement* to do so. It may turn out that a search isn't necessary or is impracticable.

Generally an officer carrying out a search has to provide details of his or her name and police station to the person searched. The officer also has to fill in a search record—this is a small form that officers carry with them.

This form shows the name or description of the person searched, along with all the other details about the search. The most important part of the form is the part where the officer has to record the *grounds* for the search. This is where the officer has to set out the reasons why he or she stopped and searched the person in the first place. The person is entitled to a copy of the search record; this can be given to them at the time of the search or at some time later within the next year.

Generally, when carrying out a search, an officer cannot require the person to remove any clothing in public other than their outer coat, jacket or gloves. However, there is a specific power for police officers to require the removal of face coverings under certain circumstances. There are also special provisions relating to the stopping and searching of people and vehicles under the Terrorism Act 2000.

Whatever the specific legal powers, the practice of stopping and searching someone who has not been arrested or convicted of anything is very delicate and those powers should be used extremely sensitively.

One of the recommendations made in the Stephen Lawrence inquiry was that the use of *any* power to stop and search members of the public (whether under PACE or any other Act) should be recorded and publicly monitored to ensure that police officers are using those powers appropriately.

Powers of entry

If you enter someone else's premises without their permission, you are a trespasser. This is a simple but important concept which you will come across later when you look at burglary. Although trespassing in this way isn't a criminal offence, it does mean that the owner can ask you to leave—and throw you out if you don't go! This general rule (which is now protected even further by the European Convention on Human Rights—see Chapter 7) applies as much to police officers as anyone else. So, if you want to go onto someone else's property you must either:

* be invited, or
* have a legal power of entry.

In some cases the owner of the property is assumed to have given general permission for people to come onto their property. This general permission usually applies to the path up to someone's front door for instance, for people who have lawful business at the house. It would be daft to expect the person delivering the post or emptying the dustbins in a particular street to go and get the specific permission of each and every householder first. This general permission applies to police officers in the same way as anyone else. It's important to note, however, that most permission to enter someone's property has some conditions attached. As one very senior judge once put it 'if I invite someone into my house for tea, I don't expect him to slide down the bannister'. If you go beyond the permission given to you by someone in their house or premises, you can again become a trespasser.

The real difficulty comes where the owner of the property not only doesn't give permission, but *wants to stop you* from entering their premises. In such cases, if you don't have a legal power to do so, you're not allowed in. Therefore, if the police didn't have any legal powers of entry they couldn't go into buildings to arrest people, to protect people, to search for things or to seize evidence.

So, as well as having powers to arrest, stop and search, the police also have powers to enter premises (and, oddly, premises usually include things like cars, caravans and boats). PACE, along with Code B of the Code of Practice, covers entry, search and seizure both with and without a warrant. As with other powers, these represent an interference with the private lives and property of individuals and therefore should be used appropriately and only where necessary.

Powers without warrant

Apart from a general power of entry to prevent a breach of the peace taking place (see Chapter 10), all other 'common law' police powers of entry were abolished by PACE. In their place, the Act introduced wide powers of entry, search and seizure for the police, particularly when made in connection with an arrest (see section 18 of PACE).

There are many Acts that give the police (and others) powers to apply for warrants; there are also many Acts which provide a power of entry without warrant. Examples are the power to enter:

* any place for the purpose of carrying out a search under the Firearms Act 1968
* school premises in connection with weapons
* relevant premises in connection with a police direction to leave and remove vehicles.

There are also other times—nothing to do with criminal activity—when police officers might need to get into someone's property quickly without asking permission first. A good example is fire. A police officer may enter and if necessary break into:

* any premises or place
* in which a fire has or is reasonably believed to have broken out.

The constable may also break into or enter:

* any premises or place
* which it is necessary to enter for the purposes of extinguishing a fire, or
* of protecting the premises for firefighting purposes, e.g. soaking things with water, breaking down doors, etc.

This power again comes from an Act of Parliament (the Fire Services Act 1947). In fact the only 'common law' power of entry without warrant (e.g. one that doesn't come from an Act of Parliament) is for dealing with a breach of the peace and only applies where officers have a genuine and reasonable belief that a breach of the peace is happening or is about to happen in the immediate future.

WEBSITE

→ www.homeoffice.gov.uk

FURTHER READING

Richard Stone, *Power of Entry, Search and Seizure*, 2003.

10

LAW AND ORDER

Police duty is pretty unusual by any standards. The motivation needed to do it, along with the training and experience it gives you, makes policing very different from most other occupations. As well as the obvious commitment, energy and resilience, a sense of compassion (and probably humour), policing requires legal powers. Different roles call for different powers and people joining the police in those different roles are taught in great detail what their respective powers are, and how and when to use them during their initial training and beyond. You have already looked at some of those powers in the earlier chapters.

Traditionally, the role of the police in England and Wales has been described as keeping law and order, but as you've seen, the role is in fact far wider and more complex than that. However, the idea of 'law and order' is quite useful because it focuses on two legal areas by which you can approach the next important area of policing—the law. This chapter gives you an introduction to some of the key concepts in criminal law; it then goes on to look at some specific aspects of police law which are mainly concerned with preserving order and keeping our communities safe.

The law

The first thing to note is that policing is not just about the criminal law: the wide range of a police officer's duties means that he or she may become involved in many different areas of law. For instance, certain types of dispute such as industrial action and picketing involve employment law, while other areas such as family law and the law relating to children, liquor licensing, betting and animals are sometimes relevant.

However, the main areas of law that concern police officers *are* found in the criminal law—and also the laws of evidence and procedure.

When dealing with criminal offences, each one can be broken down into key elements or ingredients. These are often referred to as 'points to prove' because *all* of them have to be proved before a person can be convicted. If you can't show all of the ingredients, the person has not committed that particular criminal offence. They may well have committed a *different* offence and part of the police officer's skill is recognising the different offences that can arise out of the same set of facts and circumstances.

This chapter is simply an introduction to some of the main offences and also a few basic concepts in this area—concepts that will help you if you go on to study police law in much greater detail later. If you have studied the law at school, university or in a previous job, this will act as a timely refresher.

ATTENTION TO DETAIL

It was said above that 'if you can't show all of the ingredients, the person has not committed that particular criminal offence'—this is not strictly true. The person may well have *committed* the offence but, without evidence of all the ingredients, you will not be able to *prove* that offence against them. Did you pick this point up? It is developed further on in this chapter.

As well as looking at the key ingredients of some common offences—such as theft and assault—police officers and investigators also need to consider the areas where some crimes overlap. They need to consider the range of measures that have been set out by Parliament to help tackle disorder and to create community environments where people not only are safe, but *feel* safe too. Examples are applying to the court for anti-social behaviour orders where a person's behaviour is becoming a nuisance to his or her neighbours. Naturally, a lot of time in an officer's training is spent considering the powers that the police have been given to fight crime, maintain the peace and protect life and property. As you saw in Chapter 2, the use of discretion is of great importance here, particularly when thinking of whether to use any police powers. So too is an understanding of the principles of human rights that you considered in Chapter 7.

A good working guide to the courts and the criminal justice system as seen through police eyes is *Going to Court* (see end of chapter for details).

It's a crime

What is a crime? There's no real answer to that. The classification of behaviour into 'crimes' is really an administrative matter used by police forces, the government and other organisations to measure and monitor criminal activity. The legal classification is of 'criminal offences' which are dealt with by the magistrates' courts and Crown Courts. Some criminal offences are clearly more serious than others. For instance, having the wrong sized letters on your car's number plate is a criminal offence, as is causing death by dangerous driving, but the two driving offences are totally different in terms of their consequences—both to the offender and the 'victim'.

While that doesn't necessarily mean that certain crimes are 'minor' or 'trivial' (if you want to know which crimes are 'minor' ask the victim— the answer will almost certainly be 'none'), the law has to treat some criminal offences as being of more significance than others. As a result, some offences carry greater sentences than others and require a lot more proof before someone can be convicted of them.

For these reasons the law divides criminal offences into *summary* offences and *indictable* offences.

Summary offences

Summary offences include most road traffic offences such as speeding and careless driving. However, that's not to say that there are no significant summary offences—some offences of public disorder, anti-social behaviour and drunkenness are summary offences, as are offences of taking vehicles without the owner's consent. These are common offences that can have a significant impact on people's quality of life and some are substantial criminal matters for which you can be sent to prison.

Summary offences have to be tried in the magistrates' court, either by a District Judge (a qualified and experienced lawyer) or by a bench of 'lay magistrates'—people from the community who, though not lawyers, have considerable experience in their own roles. Both lay magistrates and District Judges have powers to fine defendants or to send them to prison. About 90% of criminal cases are heard in the magistrates' courts.

Indictable offences

The other legal classification of offences is 'indictable' offences—so called because they are tried on indictment, i.e. in the Crown Court by a judge and, on most occasions, a jury.

Indictable offences are generally the offences that have the most serious consequences for victims and the community. These offences include rape, robbery, some burglaries and assaults and, of course, homicides.

In the Crown Court the judge is a qualified lawyer with many years' experience in practice and he or she is there to decide on matters of law (such as whether a piece of evidence is admissible). The jury is made up of members of the community who are there to decide questions of fact in the case—the most important one being whether the defendant is guilty!

If, having heard all the evidence that the judge allows, the jury decide that the defendant is guilty, the judge then passes sentence and has very wide powers in doing so—including the power to impose a life sentence.

So, can every criminal offence be divided into *summary* offences or *indictable* offences? The answer is 'no'—that would be far too easy. As a general rule you *can* separate offences into these two categories— offences that *must* be tried by magistrates or offences that *must* be tried by judge and jury. However, there are some offences that can be tried either way—and (helpfully) that's what they're called: 'either way' offences. These are offences where, for one reason or another, they are better off being dealt with in the magistrates' court though they could technically be brought to the Crown Court. The difference is not really of any importance at this stage, but many of the offences discussed in the rest of this chapter are 'either way' offences.

Order

One of the main duties of the police is to keep the peace and protect life and property. This has remained unchanged since the first police forces were formed. The police have a number of legal powers to help them maintain order. Probably the most important one comes from the idea of a 'breach of the peace'. This generally happens when a person is harmed or they and their property are threatened by some form of disturbance. In such situations the police can enter premises and detain anyone that is causing the disturbance or threatening the person and their property. These very important police powers come from the decisions of judges and courts over the years (known as the 'common law'), rather than in an Act of Parliament. There are criminal offences of disturbances in public places—these usually depend on the number of people present at the time. Ranging from a person making a nuisance of themselves by being offensive or drunk, up to the most serious offence of a 'riot', these situations need sensible but effective handling. Again, the police have extensive powers to deal with them.

However, the job of keeping peace, preventing crime and disorder and ensuring quality of life in the community is too vast and too important to leave to the police alone. Other public bodies, such as local authorities, also play an important part. As such, the police and local authorities regularly get together and produce a crime and disorder plan, setting out how they intend to reduce crime (and the fear of crime) in their areas. Like the police, local authorities have been given extra powers to deal with anti-social behaviour. Education authorities now have powers to exclude people from their premises and for dealing with truancy, while the courts have been given increased powers to deal with young offenders—and to make their parents more responsible for the behaviour of their offspring.

Ultimately, responsibility for ensuring law and order within the community lies with *all* the members of that community. However, the police, the courts, local authorities and other bodies can be far more effective in tackling the parts that particularly concern them where they act together.

So, back to both law and order. What follows in the next chapters is only a basic introduction to some of the key principles, but it will help to build the foundations for any later training.

FURTHER READING

Brian Fitzpatrick, *Going to Court*, 2003, Oxford: OUP.

11

A QUICK LESSON IN CRIME

There are two main reasons why, as a police officer, you need to know the ingredients of certain crimes:

* because you need to know what you will have to prove in court
* because you need to recognise if an offence has been committed in order to decide what powers are appropriate.

Even though every criminal offence is made up of its own particular ingredients, like a recipe (such as theft whose ingredients include dishonesty, the taking of someone else's property and the intention of permanently depriving the owner of it), there are some basic principles that apply in most cases.

Guilty knowledge

There is a rule in the criminal law of England and Wales that actions alone cannot amount to a crime unless they are accompanied by a 'guilty mind' or 'guilty knowledge'. The Latin term sometimes used for this guilty mind is 'mens rea'. However, the Lord Chief Justice has been working hard to stop even lawyers from using old-fashioned terminology and so no more will be said of it here.

Although there are some exceptions, it is generally safe to assume that, unless someone had the right (or wrong) intention when they carried out their criminal actions, they will not be liable for 'committing a crime'. An example of this would be theft. If you take someone else's property but, at the time, you were not being dishonest and didn't intend to keep the property, it is unlikely that a court would find you guilty. This would simply be borrowing (in the true sense). Similarly if, while out shopping today, your mind was on other things (like a new career), and you wandered out of a shop without paying for the goods you were holding, you would not have 'stolen' them. Your actions in taking the goods would not be enough to make you guilty of theft because you weren't thinking about taking them at the time. This general rule protects people who may have some mental impairment or who are not capable of understanding the consequences of their actions; it also protects people whose innocent actions go wrong—or those who just wander around shops in a daydream.

ATTENTION TO DETAIL

One common situation where people may not know what they're doing is when they are drunk. So does this mean that drunkenness amounts to 'blameless' behaviour? The answer is 'no'—if not knowing what you were doing because you were drunk gave you a general 'get out of jail free' card, how many people would ever be convicted of anything, especially serious crimes involving public order and violence? There are special rules relating to drunkenness—generally you cannot avoid conviction for most crimes simply by showing you were too drunk or too 'high' to know what you were doing (but there are some exceptions).

So what mental state *would* be enough? There are many different mental states which will meet the requirements of many different criminal offences, some of which have nothing to do with guilt or knowledge: a good example is recklessness. However, as a general rule, some degree of 'guilty mind' is needed.

Wrongful acts

The other key element that is needed is the 'wrongful act' itself. It may sound obvious but it isn't always. Simply having a guilty mind or intention can never amount to a crime on its own. If having bad thoughts were a crime, we'd all be in a lot of trouble. To prove that a person committed a crime you must show that they did the relevant guilty act as well; in our example of theft above, this would be the actual taking of the property. Other examples would include punching a victim, breaking a window or driving away a car. This element of an offence is sometimes known by its Latin name *'actus reus'* but, in order to stay on the good side of the Lord Chief Justice—and plain English—we will not use this term here.

Apart from what it's called, there's one more thing you need to note about the 'wrongful act'. In addition to showing that the person actually carried out the wrongful act, you also have to prove that they acted voluntarily—that is, that they were in control of their movements at the time. If, for example, a person is shoved into a shop window by someone else, causing the window to break, it would not be fair to blame the shoved person for causing the damage. Similarly, if you sneezed uncontrollably while you were driving and crashed into another car as a result, you should not be held responsible for driving badly.

Although it may seem obvious that you need to show that someone actually *did* something before you can convict them of a criminal offence, it is important to know that *failing to do* something can also amount to a crime. These offences are a bit more tricky. Generally, the criminal law allows people to be selfish and puts them under no duty whatsoever to help others. There is no legal duty to help a drowning person to safety or to prevent a crime being committed—and there is certainly no general duty to help the police. However, there are a few occasions where someone *will* commit a crime by failing to act. These are usually where the person concerned has a special relationship or duty towards the other person. Examples here would be where a parent fails to prevent a child from being injured or where a police officer fails to prevent an assault.

Unfinished offences

Staying with the idea of criminal acts, it is useful to look at a special group of crimes—'incomplete' or unfinished offences. These are offences where, for one reason or another, the person committing them doesn't manage to achieve what they set out to do. Consider the following example:

ATTENTION TO DETAIL

A woman puts her handbag down on a seat in a nightclub. Someone decides to try and steal a purse from inside the bag. He puts his hand into the bag only to find that there is no purse in it. The woman sees him and tells the club manager, who then calls the police and asks if an offence has been committed. If you took the club manager's call, what would you tell him?

As a starting point, take a look at the 'guilty mind and wrongful act' ingredients. In this situation, the person had the necessary guilty mind because he fully intended to steal; he also carried out the wrongful act by voluntarily putting his hand inside the bag. In fact he did everything he could to steal a purse. The fact that he was not able to steal anything was only caused by circumstances—circumstances that he was not aware of. In these circumstances the offence is said to have been an 'attempted' crime and the law treats the potential thief in the same way as if he had actually managed to steal a purse from inside the bag. This seems reasonable, given that it was only the particular circumstances of the situation that stopped him from doing what he intended.

Defences

When considering criminal offences, it is also important to think of what *defences* a person might have. A number of serious crimes have specific defences, while all have some possible form of defence. Why then do the police need to know about defences?.

There are two main reasons why police officers need to be aware of any defences that a person may have in answer to a criminal charge:

- because the police have a duty to investigate crime *impartially and fairly*—if there is evidence that supports a person's defence, the police officer should be collecting it in the same way as evidence of the offence itself; it's not their job just to collect the evidence that proves someone *did* do something wrong
- because the police will need to be able to deal with any likely defences when they interview the accused person.

Proof

'Proof' is a little word with big consequences. Remember what was said about proving criminal offences earlier in the chapter. A person can only be convicted of committing a criminal offence if there is *proof* of each ingredient of that offence against him or her. Criminal trials, like any other trials, are not about what actually happened, they're about who can prove what and for most purposes the prosecution has to prove everything.

There are only three ways of proving a person's involvement in a criminal offence:

* witnesses
* forensic evidence
* confession.

As pointed out above, it is not the job of the police simply to collect evidence *against* the accused person, nor is it their job to 'get a confession' from a suspect. The job of the police is to collect *all evidence* relating to a case impartially and efficiently, presenting it to the prosecuting authority. Although the police investigate most crime, the decision whether or not the accused person will actually be taken to court and prosecuted is not taken by the police—it is taken by the Crown Prosecution Service (CPS). It is also the CPS who will be responsible for managing the prosecution process.

In presenting the evidence against someone at a criminal trial there are several key rules to remember.

The first rule

The accused person doesn't have to prove that he or she did not commit the offence. What was once described by a famous judge as the 'golden thread' running throughout our criminal trial system is the rule that everyone is innocent unless and until they are proved guilty. You will also find this vital principle again in the European Convention on Human Rights (Article 6: see Chapter 7). Therefore it is for the CPS to prove that a person is guilty and, in doing so, we come across the second rule.

The second rule

The prosecution must present enough evidence so that the court is *sure* of the person's guilt—beyond a reasonable doubt. If the CPS don't present enough evidence for the court to be *sure*, the accused person is entitled to go free. It is not enough to show that it is *likely* that the person committed the offence or even that it is *probable*—the court has to be *sure* that the accused is guilty and nothing less will do.

Look out for victims

For every crime there is a victim—at least one, and often many more. Crime can be a fascinating subject and studying it will throw up all sorts of scenarios and variations. That is probably one reason why there are so many crime-related programmes on television. The excitement and intrigue of '*whodunnit*' has kept many a filmmaker, novelist and journalist in business as well as the real-life investigators. However, it is also important to remember the victim. Crime does not just 'happen'. It involves real people suffering real loss and having real fears. Even in what are wrongly called 'victimless' crimes by some people (such as possession of drugs and weapons) where no individual is hurt or immediately affected, there are still 'victims'. Communities and their overall well-being are often the main victims of all crime. Also, in some crimes, the person carrying out the act itself may also be a 'victim'— child prostitution is an example.

Certain groups of victims are particularly vulnerable such as those people who are too young, old or incapacitated to look after themselves. A further group is repeat victims: those people who have been targets of crime on more than one occasion. So, when you are studying the various component parts of crimes and collecting the facts, take time to consider who the *victim* might be—as well as looking for the criminal.

Continuing professional development

As a police officer, you will be given many opportunities to learn the relevant law and, most importantly, to put it into practice during your probationary period. However, it doesn't stop there. The law is constantly evolving, especially in the area of criminal justice and part of being a professional police officer involves keeping your knowledge up-to-date. It's not enough simply to pass your exams and assessments and then forget about them. Starting with the PDP and action planning described in Chapter 6, the professional development process is only the beginning. Throughout a career with the police, you will be given opportunities and support for your continuing professional development and life-long learning. Should you go on to work within a specialist department such as criminal investigation or road traffic, you will also have further training in the appropriate areas of law and procedure. If you choose to stay on patrol duties, the relevant law will be constantly changing and your training and personal development will change alongside it. The law is a 'living' instrument and it develops according to the needs of our society—it's part of a police officer's job to keep up with it.

WEBSITE

➔ www.homeoffice.gov.uk

12

LAW AND ORDER: A CLOSER LOOK

Having considered a few key legal principles in Chapter 11, it is useful to look at some specific offences in a bit more detail.

The next couple of chapters set out a number of those offences that are significant to policing, because of their frequency, seriousness or their consequences on people's quality of life—or all three.

Offences against property

A large proportion of all crimes committed in England and Wales involve property in some way. Although the statistics show that the number of these crimes is falling, they still account for the vast majority of reported crimes. Theft of property accounts for over half of all recorded crime. However, property crime does not only cover the stealing of other people's things; it also covers damaging and destroying property, breaking into homes, shops and schools and also taking motor vehicles. As you have seen, the peaceful enjoyment of your property is a fundamental human right which is protected by the European Convention (see Chapter 7).

Property crime is the cause of a great deal of misery and distress. Not only does it bring unhappiness and expense to the people whose property has been stolen or damaged, property crime also:

* has an enormous impact on the economy
* creates fear of crime in the community

- uses up a considerable amount of police time and resources.

Some property crimes—such as burglary—can include injury or harm to the occupier of property as well. As a result of all the above features, most property crimes carry substantial prison sentences.

So let's look at some of the main property crimes.

Theft

A good starting point when looking at property crime is theft. Most people already have a rough idea of what is involved in theft—in fact most societies the world over have some offence to stop people taking other people's property. Apart from a few technical matters that you will come across later in your training, the crime of theft is pretty straight-forward. If you were guessing what the ingredients of theft are, what would you say?

The ingredients are as follows.

Dishonesty

This is simply what it says; if a person behaved in a way that would generally be seen by others as 'dishonest', that will usually be enough.

Appropriation

Although many thefts involve *taking* something, the word 'taking' is not really wide enough to cover all situations so Parliament came up with 'appropriating' instead. Generally, 'appropriating' something is like taking it.

Property

It seems obvious but you can only commit theft if there is something to steal. The only complicating bit here is that not all things count as 'property'. So, for instance, you cannot 'steal' land (for reasons that are not really interesting or important here). Other things that cannot be stolen include electricity and there are special rules for flowers and fruit when growing wild (don't worry why). Some less obvious things that *are* 'property' for the purposes of theft include the balance from a bank account, copyright in a video recording and shares in a company.

Belonging to another

Again this might seem obvious but the property stolen must belong to someone else. There are a few situations where you can be guilty of stealing your own property (but you can ignore them for now); however, generally the property must belong to somebody other than the person who 'appropriated' or took it.

Intention of permanently depriving

This is probably the key part of theft. If someone dishonestly takes your property but intends to give it back later, this is not theft. For this reason, there is a particular crime which deals with taking other people's cars for a ride and then abandoning them (see below). For there to be a theft, there must be a clear intention by the thief to deprive the owner of their property for ever.

If any one of the above ingredients is missing, there is no crime of theft (though there may well be any number of other crimes).

At this point an example may help.

EXAMPLE

Petra, a college student, runs out of milk. She sees some bottles of milk on the doorstep of the house across the road. As she has no money at that time, Petra takes the milk from her neighbours' doorstep, intending

continued

---

continued

to replace it with some other milk later that day. Someone sees Petra taking the milk and calls the police. If you were the police officer what would you do?

There are several issues to think about here. You now know that the ingredients of the crime of theft are dishonestly appropriating property that belongs to someone else with the intention of permanently depriving the other person of the property. The first problem is whether or not Petra was 'dishonest'. If she knows the neighbours well, it might be that she thinks they would have let her have the milk if she had asked them. On the other hand, they may dislike her and might have refused to help her—which might be why she didn't ask them. The fact that Petra intends to replace the milk later will not necessarily help her here. We can see that she has 'appropriated' or taken the milk and also that milk is clearly property belonging to someone else. As she intends to use the milk, that would mean that Petra intends to deprive the neighbours of it permanently; even if she replaces it later, it will not be the same milk that she took. So, has she committed theft?

Robbery

Now that you understand theft, you are also most of the way to understanding robbery. People sometimes use the term 'robbing' in relation to shops, cars and houses. They will say 'I've had my car robbed' or 'they robbed her house last week'. However, in fact (and law) you can only rob *people*. Robbery is simply a theft which is accompanied by violence or threats of violence to a person. If there is no theft, there is no robbery.

Robbery can range from mobile phone snatches where force or threats are used towards the owner, to armed hold-ups of banks and security vans. The key additional ingredient here is the use of force or the threat of immediate force against someone else present at the scene. There is no need to use a weapon and there is no special offence of armed robbery or 'robbery with violence' (though this will affect sentence at court).

Robbery is a very serious offence and can only be tried in the Crown Court.

Burglary

Just as only *people* can be robbed, only *buildings* can be burgled. Again this is something that people generally mix up, talking of their cars being burgled. In his best-selling book, *The Clothes They Stood Up In*, Alan Bennett makes the point clear:

> the Ransomes had been burgled. 'Robbed', Mrs Ransome said. 'Burgled', Mr Ransome corrected. Premises were burgled; persons were robbed. (*The Clothes They Stood Up In*, Alan Bennett, 1998, London: Profile Books)

Burglary is more complicated than theft or robbery; in fact it's more complicated than most offences. However, there are some key features that, once you understand them, will make everything clear—in theory . . .

First, there are two types of burglary: one deals with the burglar's intentions at the time he or she enters a building, while the other deals with the burglar's behaviour once inside the building. Grasp this and it's pretty well downhill from here.

Type 1: intentions

The ingredients for the first type of burglary are:

* Entering a building (or part of a building)—this can include reaching an arm through an open window or leaning through a door

* as a trespasser—if you don't have permission to enter, you're a trespasser. Trespassing is rarely a crime in itself (so all those signs that say 'trespassers will be prosecuted' are usually an empty threat). It is worth noting that general permission is given to people to enter certain buildings such as shops, museums and hospitals. This permission will, however, be limited to certain areas and certain times (like the sales floor in a shopping mall during opening hours). Remember the judge sliding down the banisters? If not, go back to Chapter 9. If a person enters either a place to which the permission does not apply (like a storeroom) or enters at a time when they shouldn't be there (say, after the shop has closed), they will be a trespasser

* intending to do one or more of four acts, i.e.—

  * steal
  * inflict serious injury on anyone inside
  * rape anyone inside
  * cause damage.

Note that this is a crime of *intention*; the burglar does not actually have to carry out any theft, rape etc.—it is enough that he or she intended to do so at the time they entered the building as a trespasser. Think of how you would try to prove to a court that someone had intended to do one of the four acts. Things such as preparation, any previous threats they had made to people. Similarly, anything that they may have had with them (e.g. sledgehammers, spray paint, knives) would be good evidence. There is also a further, very serious, crime of 'aggravated' burglary where burglars have certain weapons with them. Of course, if the burglar *does* go on to carry out one of the four acts then this is very good evidence of their intention. If they go on to *steal* or to *inflict serious injury* on someone inside the building, they commit the second type of burglary.

Type 2: behaviour after entering

The second type of burglary is concerned with what the person did *after entering* the building or part of the building. If the person, having entered as a trespasser, steals anything (or tries to) or inflicts serious injury on anyone inside (or tries to), they commit this offence.

You can see that there is a big overlap between these two types of burglary and often both have been committed on the same facts. Another example may be needed:

EXAMPLE

A man who has gone into a pub for a drink with friends visits the toilets. He hides in the toilets until the pub has closed, when he goes back into the bar room and takes a bottle of whisky and some cigarettes from behind the bar. The landlord hears a noise from the bar area and calls the police. If you are the police officer, what do you do?

The starting point in deciding whether the man has committed either type of burglary is whether or not he was a *trespasser*. At the time he went into the toilets the man was a customer of the pub and had permission to be there—like all the other people using the pub. So he wasn't trespassing. However, once the pub closed, the man no longer had this permission and he became a trespasser. Although he had not entered the toilets as a trespasser, he was certainly a trespasser when he entered *the bar area*. At this point, if he had intended to do one of the four acts (theft, serious injury, rape or damage) he would be guilty of burglary—the first type. When he takes the drinks and cigarettes he dishonestly appropriates property belonging to the landlord, intending to deprive him permanently of it. We know this is theft, so the man is also guilty of the second type of burglary.

ATTENTION TO DETAIL

Did you realise that, even if the pub had still been open when he took the property, the man did not have any permission to go *behind the bar* and therefore he was a trespasser at this point anyway?

Burglary is a serious offence that can have considerable impact on the victims—especially if the 'building' involved is their home. It is worth remembering what was said earlier about victims of crime at this point; many victims of domestic burglary are 'repeat' victims—that is, they have been burgled more than once. The effect of burglary on people's feeling of security, and that of their families and children can be devastating. Burglary of homes is treated by the courts as a particularly serious crime.

Taking vehicles

That's buildings dealt with. What about vehicles? Of course, vehicles are property and so can be stolen like any other property. However, as you saw in the discussion above, just because someone takes another's property there will not necessarily be a crime of theft. Some vehicles such as mobile homes can also be 'buildings' for the purposes of burglary, but these occasions are too rare to worry about here.

An example may help as a reminder of the principles of theft:

EXAMPLE

Two youths see a super-charged car in a multi-storey car park late one evening. Never having driven one of these cars before, they break into it, remove the steering lock and start the engine with the ignition wires. The youths drive around the car park for a while then, becoming more adventurous, drive out into the main road system and race up and down a dual carriageway. After half an hour the car runs out of petrol. The youths abandon it at the side of the road and run off. A passing post office worker sees where they went and rings the police, giving the address of a house that the youths went into. If you are the police officer, what do you do?

Working through the theft ingredients, you will have identified that the youths were dishonest, that they appropriated (took) the car and that the car belonged to someone else. What is missing is the final element—the intention of *permanently depriving* the owner of the car, so they haven't stolen it. What the youths have done is taken the car without the owner's permission—and that's the next offence.

ATTENTION TO DETAIL

Did you pick up on the fact that, although they have not stolen the car itself, they have dishonestly used up the owner's petrol with the intention of permanently depriving the owner of it—they have therefore technically stolen the *petrol*. This is a very technical point and, if you did notice this your investigative future is looking good!

Taking vehicles is known by many names in different parts of the country and across different police forces: 'Unlawful Taking of Motor

Vehicles' (UTMV), 'Taking and Driving Away' (TDA) and 'Taking Without the Owner's Consent' (TWOC). Another name—the worst—given by some newspapers is 'joyriding'. In fact there is little to be joyous about and this offence creates fear, frustration and further expense to the community—not to mention the considerable risk to life. You may have been the victim of this offence yourself; if not, you will almost certainly have seen abandoned cars sporting their 'Police Aware' stickers by the side of the road. There is a further, aggravated, form of this offence that occurs where the vehicle is involved in certain other incidents before the owner gets it back. This carries a longer sentence at court.

The key element to remember in this offence is the 'consent of the owner'. If the person taking the car asks permission first, the offence is not committed. Similarly, where the person taking the car believes that if:

* they had asked the owner, and
* *had told the owner of the circumstances*

the owner would have given permission, the offence is not committed.

What does this mean? Let's take another example.

EXAMPLE

A police officer at a Police Training Centre usually allows her colleague to use her motor bike to go to a local gym every Tuesday and Thursday. One Tuesday the colleague cannot find the owner of the motor bike so he takes it anyway. After all, he only wants it to go to the gym and the owner usually lets him use it for this purpose. The owner comes back and finds that the bike is missing. She calls another police officer for advice—you. What do you tell her?

First, has the colleague taken a motor vehicle? The answer is 'yes'. Next, has he got the owner's consent first? The answer is 'not specifically'. However, he believes that if he had asked her if he could use the bike to go to the gym, she would have said 'yes'. For this reason he does not commit the offence of taking a conveyance without the owner's consent—even though he has taken her vehicle without asking. However, If he had taken the other officer's new Mini to use in a cross-country rally, that is a different matter altogether.

Also, as a final note, it is an offence to get a lift with someone when you know that they have taken the conveyance without the owner's consent.

Going equipped

Generally the criminal law is aimed at preventing crime taking place, as well as providing offences and police power to deal with crime once it has happened. Therefore, in addition to creating the above offences to protect property and its owners, the law also makes it an offence to have articles for use in the course of burglary, theft or deception. 'Articles' here will mean anything that a person intends to use in the course of a burglary, theft or deception offence. Examples would be screwdrivers for breaking into cars and houses, knives or weapons for threatening occupiers and even balaclavas, disguises and false identity documents that the person intends to use to commit these offences. If you can prove that the person did in fact intend to use the article in committing any of those offences *and* that he or she had the article with them when they were away from their home address, they commit the offence of 'going equipped'. There is no need to show that the person actually went on to commit an offence of burglary, theft or deception and the whole point of this offence is to allow the police and the courts to deal with people *before* the property offence has been committed.

Criminal damage

We have already seen how people are given a right to the peaceful enjoyment of their property under the European Convention on Human Rights (Protocol 1, Article 1 to be precise—see Chapter 7). The protection of that right can be seen in the property offences considered above. However, it also extends to protecting the property from damage and there are several criminal offences that arise from damaging property. The law here doesn't just stop you from damaging other people's property; it also prevents you from damaging *your own* property under certain circumstances. That's not quite as odd as it might sound. Have a look at the legislation.

The main law containing the relevant offences is found in the Criminal Damage Act 1971. While it may seem obvious that it is an offence to damage some else's property, the Act also makes it an offence to damage or destroy *your own property* (or someone else's) under circumstances where you are endangering someone's life. An example of this would be if someone chopped down a 15 metre high tree in their garden and the tree was likely to fall into a busy road. Burning your own property in a way that is likely to endanger someone else would be another example.

The Act also makes it an offence to:

* *threaten* to damage or destroy property
* have articles to be used for damaging or destroying property and to
* commit an offence which is 'racially or religiously aggravated'.

So making a threat to come round and smash up someone's home or possessions is an offence in itself, as is having an aerosol can to go and spray graffiti or having a felt pen for writing on a bus shelter.

Just as there are times when you can't damage your own property, there are also times where you *are* allowed to damage someone else's property. Such occasions are usually where it is necessary to cause the damage in order to protect property or human life, or where the owner of the property has given you permission (or would have given you permission if they had known of the situation).

An example may help again.

EXAMPLE

During a hot summer day a motorist accidentally locks their pet dog in their car. While the motorist is away from the car seeking help, a member of the public sees the animal in the car and tells you, a police officer, that they are worried about the animal. What do you do?

As a starting point, if you tried to force the car's door or to insert something into the lock or door surround, you would be in danger of causing 'damage'. Damage includes scratching or defacing property to even a small degree. However, if you chose to break into the car window in order to save the dog you might be able to claim a defence, by showing either that the damage was necessary to protect the dog from harm or that the owner would have given you permission to break the window if they had known about it. This second element is similar to the 'consent' issue that you considered earlier in this chapter in relation to taking someone's vehicle.

ATTENTION TO DETAIL

In the above situation, the dog is itself 'property' for the purposes of criminal damage. This can seem a strange concept at first but, so far as the law is concerned, even living things such as domestic pets, farm

continued

continued

animals and plants are property and can therefore be 'damaged'. Also, just to confuse, some things don't count as property for the purposes of criminal damage like flowers and foliage of plants *growing wild*—if they've been grown in someone's garden or public flower bed, they are 'property'.

'Aggravated damage' happens where the person damages property and intends to endanger someone's life or is reckless as to whether someone's life is endangered. An example of this very serious offence would be where a person throws a brick through the window of a moving car. In many offences of 'aggravated damage', fire is also involved. Setting fire to a house or a shop would almost always be 'aggravated damage'; causing any damage by fire is known as arson. The most serious form of criminal damage is aggravated damage by arson—this carries life imprisonment.

Racially or religiously aggravated offences

Some offences—not just damage—are treated as being particularly unpleasant because they are motivated by racism. Even before the report into the murder of Stephen Lawrence, there was considerable concern at the additional evil of crimes that were specifically aimed at racial groups or motivated by hostility towards a person's racial origins.

The authors of the Stephen Lawrence Report said that:

We believe that the use of the words 'racial' and 'racially motivated' are in themselves inaccurate because we all belong to one human race, regardless of our colour, culture or ethnic origin . . .

As a result, the inquiry recommended a new definition of a *'racist incident'*, namely 'any incident which is perceived to be racist by the victim or any other person'.

That definition was adopted by police forces around England and Wales for the purposes of reporting and recording crime but it does not yet appear in any legislation. The Crime and Disorder Act 1998 (passed before the report of the Stephen Lawrence inquiry) re-visited the whole issue of racially aggravated crime and this was itself extended even further after the events of 11 September 2001 to include *religiously* aggravated crimes. The result was the identification of a number of offences that would be treated as being far more serious by the police and the courts if they are shown to have been *racially or religiously aggravated*. How would that be shown? Generally an offence will be racially or religiously aggravated if:

• at the time of committing it (or immediately before/after), the person demonstrates towards the victim hostility based on the victim's membership of a racial or religious group, or

• the offence is motivated by hostility towards members of a racial or religious group based on their membership of that group.

Criminal damage is one of the named offences that can be racially or religiously aggravated. The other offences that can be aggravated by racial or religious considerations in this way include assaults and woundings and some offences against the public peace—and these general areas of law and order are the next to be considered.

Offences against people

The next group of offences to consider are those committed directly against people. Generally these are categorised according to the amount of injury that the assailant caused or intended to cause to their victim. You may already be familiar with some of the names used for these offences such as 'grievous bodily harm' for instance.

Most of the main offences against people involve assaults (and also what is technically known as battery—the actual application of physical force). If unlawful force (or a real threat of it) is used towards another person, an offence will have been committed. Most offences against people are found in an old Act of Parliament, the Offences Against the Person Act 1861. The exception to this is the first level of assault, called common assault, which is contained in the Criminal Justice Act 1988. Common assault covers assaults that don't cause significant or lasting physical injury. A slap across the face or a kick in the shins would be examples. While it's true that normal day-to-day life will involve knocking against other people—say on crowded commuter trains or in clubs or bars—these types of activity are not considered to be assaults. Any deliberate unwanted touching or application of physical force going beyond these everyday matters will potentially be common assaults. If a common assault is carried out in circum-stances of indecency (e.g. an uninvited feeling of someone's genital area) it becomes an 'indecent assault', a wholly different type of offence and one which is beyond the scope of this book. There are also specific offences of common assault against police officers and designated and accredited personnel such as Police Community Support Officers.

If the force used brings about greater injury, such as a black eye or a broken tooth, this is likely to be an 'assault occasioning actual bodily harm' or section 47 assault (as it's contained in section 47 of the Offences Against the Person Act 1861). If the force used causes signifi-cant or serious harm, such as a wound or a broken limb, this will be 'grievous bodily harm or wounding' (under section 20 of the Act). Both actual bodily harm and grievous bodily harm can involve *psychological* injury as well as physical injury and carry maximum sentences of five years' imprisonment. All three levels of assault can be 'racially or religiously aggravated' (see above). If so, they will attract a heavier sentence from the courts. Also, if the assailant *intended* to cause that level of harm or injury, the law (under section 18 of the 1861 Act) treats the offence as even more serious and provides a penalty of life imprisonment.

Finally, if a person is killed as the result of the assault, the relevant offence will be homicide. Homicide is divided into two offences—murder and manslaughter. Murder is committed where the assailant intended to kill the victim or cause them grievous bodily harm and manslaughter is covered by a wide variety of other circumstances where the assailant did not have that relevant intention. It is perhaps surprising that homicide is not covered by the Offences Against the Person Act 1861—or any other Act for that matter. It is a common law offence, developed by the courts over the centuries.

EXAMPLE

Krask is walking through a crowded bar carrying two drinks. He accidentally brushes against a woman and then bumps into a man, knocking the man's leg against a table. Another man walking towards the bar tries to take the glasses from Krask for a joke but Krask doesn't find it amusing and kicks the man on the leg. The man swears at Krask who then head-butts him in the face breaking one of his teeth. Krask then hits the man with one of the glasses he is carrying, causing it to break and cutting the man's cheek open. At what point does Krask commit offences of assault and what types of assault are they?

Following this clumsy and aggressive character through the crowd may help to illustrate the law of assaults.

ATTENTION TO DETAIL

Krask is walking through a crowded bar carrying two drinks. He accidentally brushes against a woman. At this point, although he has made unwanted contact with the woman, there is no suggestion that Krask intended to assault her (indecently or otherwise) and this is simply everyday contact expected in normal life. *Krask then bumps into a man, knocking the man's leg against a table.* Here again, although he's caused the man to bump his leg, Krask's actions appear to be within the normal hustle and bustle of a crowded bar. Therefore there is no assault. *Another man walking towards the bar tries to take the glasses from Krask for a joke but Krask doesn't find it amusing and kicks the man on the leg.* This is the first point at which he commits an assault. Here Krask applies unlawful physical force to someone else. As he doesn't cause any real injury, the assault is probably a common assault. *The man swears at Krask who then headbutts him in the face breaking one of his teeth.* This action is clearly an assault—and as it causes a broken tooth, it is probably actual bodily harm. *Krask then hits the man with one of the glasses he is carrying, causing it to break and cutting the man's cheek open.* Krask has now added wounding or grievous bodily harm to his list of offences against the person.

Offences against the peace

This is a slightly misleading heading. In pure legal terms, offences against the peace mean common law offences generally. However, this is not a legal textbook and the label is a useful one covering a number of important offences that all have one common feature—the disturbance of people's peaceful enjoyment of their private, public or community life. So we'll stick with it.

The starting point here is a breach of the peace. This concept was introduced in Chapter 11. A breach of the peace is not an offence itself, but you can be arrested for it and bound over to keep the peace by a magistrates' court. You have also seen how someone's behaviour can amount to a number of different offences being committed. There are several criminal offences that are committed where someone goes beyond a simple breach of the peace and uses threatening, abusive or insulting words or behaviour, or other conduct causing harassment, alarm or distress. These offences are generally referred to as public order offences and, helpfully, most are contained in the Public Order Act 1986.

Public disorder

The most serious public order offences are riot and violent disorder. These are committed where more than one person is involved in concerted acts of violence or threatened violence. Riot involves 12 or more people while violent disorder involves three or more people acting together: both are arrestable offences (and if you've forgotten what these are, go back to Chapter 8).

The next level of public disorder is the offence of affray. This occurs where a person uses or threatens unlawful violence towards another person and this conduct would cause a person of reasonable firmness present at the scene to fear for his or her personal safety. An affray carries a specific power of arrest for police officers to use and attracts a maximum penalty of three years' imprisonment. There then follow a series of offences involving threatening, abusive or insulting words or behaviour. If someone uses words or behaviour which:

* are intended or likely to cause someone to fear the use of immediate unlawful violence, or

* are intended to cause someone harassment, alarm or distress

they will commit other offences under the Public Order Act 1986, each of which carries a specific power of arrest for police officers. These offences can also be racially or religiously aggravated, attracting heavier sentences.

Offensive and anti-social behaviour

In addition to the major public order offences above, there are several other offences which, though attracting lesser penalties, address causes of considerable disquiet within communities.

Using threatening, abusive or insulting words or behaviour, or disorderly behaviour within the hearing or sight of a person likely to be caused harassment, alarm or distress is itself an offence (and one that can be racially/religiously aggravated). There is a further, general, offence of anti-social behaviour for which police officers will have a power of arrest. Police Community Support Officers as well as constables will also have a power to demand the name and address of anyone behaving in an anti-social manner.

An extra measure that is available to the police (in conjunction with the local authority) is the anti-social behaviour order or ASBO. This is an order that can be made by the courts preventing an individual from engaging in anti-social conduct in the future—whether that person has been convicted of any particular offence or not. If a person breaches an ASBO they will commit an offence and can be arrested. Similar orders are available in respect of convicted sex offenders.

There are also several offences that have been listed as being particularly common—and particularly disruptive to the public peace. As such, these offences have been singled out as being suitable to be dealt with by issuing fixed penalty notices, both by constables and other designated or accredited personnel. In summary, these offences are:

- using threatening, abusive or insulting words or behaviour
- throwing stones at trains
- dropping litter
- making nuisance telephone calls
- wasting police time.

Drunkenness

There is a particular offence of being drunk and disorderly and all that needs to be proved is that the person was disorderly, while drunk, in a public place. This offence carries a power of arrest for anyone (every citizen and police personnel). Additionally, the police have other powers to deal with situations where there is a potential for drunkenness or other anti-social behaviour involving drink. For instance, there is a power under the Confiscation of Alcohol (Young Persons) Act 1997. This power says that, where a constable reasonably suspects that a person in a 'relevant place' is in possession of alcoholic drink (intoxicating liquor) and that either:

- the person is under the age of 18, or
- the person intends that any of that drink should be drunk by a person under the age of 18 in that or any other relevant place, or
- a person under the age of 18 who is (or has recently been) with him or her has recently drunk alcohol in that or any other relevant place,

the constable may require the person to surrender anything in their possession which is, or which the constable reasonably believes to be, alcoholic drink and to state his or her name and address. Some of these powers can be given to designated auxiliary staff as well.

Relevant places here are public places or places where the person has gained entry unlawfully.

There are further offences and powers that allow the police and other auxiliary staff to deal with drunkenness in areas that have been specially designated by the local authority. You may have seen notices specifying places such as parks and shopping precincts for this purpose. More senior police officers have additional powers to order premises to be closed where there is anti-social behaviour involving the sale of alcohol.

Offences against policy

Some criminal offences aren't really committed *against* any particular person or property. These are sometimes called 'victimless' crimes, an unhelpful expression that ignores the wider consequences of crime. Crime always has a victim, whether that victim is a person, a group of people or the community in general.

So a new category of offence is probably needed here and the one chosen for the purposes of this book is that of offences against policy as decided by the elected government of the day. These offences cover various areas of criminal law, for instance some sexual offences where the parties are all consenting. The best everyday policing examples though are in the two main areas of drugs and weapons.

Controlled drugs

The misuse of controlled drugs has become such a real feature of our society that it now touches almost every aspect of community life. Its impact on crime and community safety has become so significant that it is one of the most frequently encountered areas of criminal law for police officers.

Before going on to consider the principal offences involving drugs, it is first necessary to understand the key concept of 'controlled drugs'.

The list of controlled drugs has developed almost as fast as the substances themselves.

You will find the precise chemical names of the drugs in the Misuse of Drugs Act 1971. Unfortunately the Act does not refer to the relevant street names of the drugs by which they're more likely to be known (to both the police and the offender) but the important classification is that of Class A, B or C drugs. The classes are made generally on the basis of each drug's potential effects on both the person taking it and society in general and classification is important in determining the sentencing powers of the courts. The whole issue of drugs classes attracted acres of newspaper space recently over the proposed re-classification of cannabis.

Class A drugs include the most notorious and dangerous drugs such as heroin and morphine, cocaine, some amphetamines, ecstasy and LSD. Class B includes codeine and some amphetamines—it has also contained cannabis and cannabis resin though this is going to change. Cannabis and cannabis resin will become Class C drugs alongside some commonly-abused prescription drugs. As such cannabis will still be a controlled drug and its use will *not* have been legalised or de-criminal-ised—despite what the media may lead you to believe. What *will* have changed is that the sentences that the courts can give for some offences involving those drugs will be reduced, simple possession will no longer be an arrestable offence and the police priorities in detecting and pros-ecuting those offences will be affected. This is very different from saying that you can no longer be arrested for possessing cannabis; if you're not sure why, go back to Chapter 8.

A recent study showed that the total economic cost of Class A drug use alone in England and Wales is £3.5 billion, with the total social consequences of Class A drug use equal to £12 billion (Home Office Research Study, No. 249).

The main offences involving controlled drugs can be divided into:

* simple possession—where the drug is intended for personal use or no other purpose can be proved
* possession intending to supply someone else with the drug
* supplying or offering to supply someone else with a drug.

The penalties and police powers in relation to offences of simple possession are less than in the case of the other two levels of offence— but that doesn't stop them from being criminal offences. It is an offence to possess controlled drugs even for purely personal use. The most serious drugs offences are those where the drug involved is a Class A drug and the person intends to supply other people with it or to import it into the United Kingdom.

In practical terms, police officers are unlikely to be able to identify a particular drug if it is in tablet or powder form and therefore many drug arrests are made on suspicion. There are other offences involving the production and importation of controlled drugs but these are outside the scope of this book.

Weapons

The carrying of weapons has become an issue of considerable concern over recent years. In particular, the use of knives in crime has caused some notable changes in the law. For these reasons, the powers to stop and search people that were discussed in Chapter 9 were made available to the police in relation to weapons.

Generally the law makes a distinction between knives and similar articles and other sorts of weapons. Firearms are a particular group of weapons that attract very strict controls and these are outside the scope of this book, though, as a rule, it will be an offence for most people to have handguns, rifles, shotguns and ammunition for any of them unless they have specific authority to do so.

Although you may be familiar with terms such as 'offensive weapon', the law in this area is wide and complex, going far beyond simply making it an offence to have such items. Some legislation is aimed at preventing the *carrying* of certain weapons and other items, while in other areas it is concerned with other behaviour such as the sale or use of weapons.

Generally, though, it is offence (an *arrestable offence*: see Chapter 8) to have any offensive weapon in a public place without lawful authority or reasonable excuse.

What is an offensive weapon? An offensive weapon is something that is made, adapted or intended for causing injury to someone else. Examples of something *made* for causing injury would be a police baton or a bayonet. An example of something *intended* for causing injury might be a Stanley knife that a person takes out with them in order to attack a victim. Likewise, something *adapted* is just what it says—an example would be home-made weapons such as broken bottles or sharpened sticks.

EXAMPLE

Police officers carrying batons or members of the armed forces carrying bayonets on parade have offensive weapons with them in public places. However, they have 'lawful authority' here. Similarly, people having tools with them in the course of their work (e.g. craft knives for fitting carpets or hammers for joinery) might have a 'reasonable excuse' for having these items in public as long as they didn't intend to use them for causing injury.

This is the basic offence and it is 'arrestable'. But there are further arrestable offences where there is no need to show that the weapon was made, adapted or intended to cause injury. There is an offence preventing the carrying of knives or other bladed or sharply pointed instruments in public (or on school premises) without good reason or lawful authority. There is an exception for small pen-knives provided the cutting edge of the blade is not longer than 7.62 cm (3 inches), but the offence is generally much wider than the offensive weapons offences above. Sharply pointed instruments will include *anything* fitting that description: hat pins, sharpened sticks, darts, etc.

Once again, the law here overlaps and there may be a need to consider more than one possible offence arising out of the same behaviour.

ATTENTION TO DETAIL

If a person is found to have a sharpened stick with them in the street there may be a number of offences that are relevant. Having been sharpened, the stick could be seen as an 'offensive weapon' by the courts. However, the person may also intend to use the stick to injure someone else—also making it an offensive weapon. As the stick is a sharply-pointed article, the person may commit the other offence but, in either case, he might have lawful authority for his actions.

In addition to the controls on the carrying of weapons, there are also restrictions on the sale, manufacture, hire and buying of some weapons. The legislation is aimed at restricting the supply of such weapons and their availability in England and Wales. The restrictions cover various types of knives—including knives disguised as other objects—and also specialist martial arts equipment such as *shuriken* throwing stars and fighting claws. There are specific offences involving the sale of knives to people under 16 and also to the advertising and marketing of knives. Crossbows have their own legislation and police powers for seizure.

FURTHER READING

The Economic and Social Costs of Class A Drug Use in England and Wales 2000, Home Office Research Study No. 249.

R Matthews and J Pitts, *Crime, Disorder and Community Safety*, 2001, London: Routledge.

Crawford, *Crime Prevention and Community Safety: Policies, Politics and Practices*, 1998, Longman.

13

COMMUNICATING

Language, labels and loose talk

Language is so fundamental to our way of life that it is one of the first things we begin to learn—at least our first language. Like many aspects of life that are learned passively and picked up along the way, the language and words we use are often adopted without a great deal of consideration. Ways of describing and expressing things become a habit, developed in families, school and other social settings. Within policing this has two main effects. On the one hand, the policing world has a language all of its own, a language which officers pick up from others and which unites them, allowing them to discuss things in a quicker or more specific way—in the same way as many occupations such as the armed forces, transport workers, and (especially) the IT industry. This involves attaching 'labels' to certain objects, events or situations—often in the form of acronyms or abbreviations. Communicating in this way can be seen as a type of *inclusionary* language in that it *includes* everyone in that particular job or workplace. Provided it is 'appropriate' (i.e. not offensive or divisive), this language can be a positive thing and the second half of this chapter looks at some 'police speak' in more detail.

The other effect of the way in which first languages are learned and adopted is less positive. Some expressions or words that are used all the time within one particular group or setting can offend other people who are from another group or setting—and some 'labels' are entirely inappropriate. That doesn't mean that the person using certain words or expressions always *intends* them to be offensive or to cause someone else discomfort—in fact it's often quite the opposite. Like some of the weapons considered in the last chapter, they can still be offensive, even though you didn't intend them to be. An example is the use of the word 'coloured' when referring to people from certain ethnic groups. To some people this might be seen as a 'polite' or considerate way of making reference to what they see as a sensitive issue—skin colour. To others it may be seen as offensive because of its historical connections or simply because it's clumsy and inaccurate—and why use a 'label' focusing on someone's skin colour at all? Is skin colour *relevant* to the conversation or discussion?

Labelling

Labelling in the above way is usually irrelevant and always unnecessary. However, it's hard habit to break. Labelling things is a critical part of learning to make sense of the world around us; if you've worked with, or brought up children you'll have seen how this works. So too is 'stereotyping'—putting things into groups and giving them names (e.g. animals, buildings, features of the weather). Again, you will see from the second part of this chapter that the police—like other professionals— have given specific names to lots of things that crop up in their every-day working roles. However, labelling and stereotyping can be highly inappropriate—particularly where it's *people* who are being labelled. Categorising people in this way also makes a lot of assumptions, most or all of which may not be true of *every* person in that group. This is a particularly sensitive issue where the use of police powers—such as those to stop and search people—is concerned. Police officers cannot single people out for search, arrest or questioning solely on the basis that they think someone looks like a 'typical' criminal, neither can they single them out in this way because they have a certain lifestyle (such as travellers).

ATTENTION TO DETAIL

A man telephones his local police station to report his child missing. The child has been missing for several hours and the man is obviously very concerned. The Control Room staff take the child's details and pass them to the senior detective on duty. On receiving the details the Detective says: *'Oh no—that's my son!'*

Where's the problem? There isn't one—as long as you didn't *assume* that the Detective was a man. It might be that you've seen similar examples to this before but it makes the point.

Police officers themselves suffer from labelling and stereotyping. There are plenty of labels for police officers, most of them derogatory; there are also police stereotypes such as the cheery plodding 'music hall' constable. Labels and stereotypes such as these assume that all people in the group are identical.

So where's the list of words that shouldn't be used or should be avoided? There isn't one. You could make a list of the more obvious words and expressions that will almost certainly cause offence. However, the problem is not so much knowing what words and expressions may be upsetting to someone, but being sensitive to *all* the words you are using in a given situation. Because the language we develop is so fundamental to our personal lives, using words and expressions becomes second-nature. The answer is in developing sensitivity in your use of language.

> **ATTENTION TO DETAIL**
>
> In his novel, *The Liar*, Stephen Fry warns that words are indeed like weapons—and, if you don't check to see if a word is loaded before you use it, don't be surprised when it goes off in your face!

One good thing about the English language is that there is always at least one other word which will do the job just as well as the one you're not sure about. If you're worried that a certain word, phrase or expression may be inappropriate—use another one.

Police officers receive in-depth training in developing language and communication skills in general, and in their approach to diversity in particular. This is not just an exercise in 'political correctness'; you will have seen from the Competency Framework earlier (see Chapter 3) that communicating appropriately is a core skill of effective policing.

Language that *includes*

Like many jobs, the police service has its own informal language. Whatever your own first language, you will also learn a whole new vocabulary in the police service. Within this vocabulary, many shorthand expressions have developed in the police setting. Made of mainly of letters, nicknames and abbreviations—and even numbers—this police speak or cop talk can be very confusing to everyone when they first come across it. Take this police station conversation for instance:

EXAMPLE

Constable Birts: *'What happened with that ABH job the other night Azz? Started off with just a HORTI didn't it?'*

Constable Azziz: *'Don't ask! And it wasn't a HORTI—It was a routine MFH to start with—a kid in the back of a car with an older driver. I was about to do a PNC check when he suddenly went daft. And it wasn't an ABH either. I'd have said it was a section 18 or at least a good 20. SOCO thought so as well. Anyway, CPS advice reckons it's not even a 47. He was 47(3) bailed and now he's only looking at a section 39.*

Confused? Not surprising really. But it's pretty straightforward. You will find a rough and ready glossary below to help decode some of the police speak you may hear. Try using it to make at least some sense of the above conversation.

Although the list below contains some of the more common references used in the police, just to complicate things, some expressions differ from one force to another, while others are probably best left out altogether!

Terminology

Who?	*What?*
ACPO	Association of Chief Police Officers. All chief officers from Home Office police forces and the chief officers of the Police Service for Northern Ireland belong to ACPO. It provides many different advisory committees (e.g. on firearms, training, crime, etc.) and contributes to debates on

important issues such as drugs policies, sex offenders and the like.

ACPOS	Same as ACPO but for Scotland
ACPOD	Nothing like ACPO. Association of Chief Police Officers' Drivers.
ACSO	Accredited Community Support Officer
APA	Association of Police Authorities
BPA	Black Police Association. Provides support and advice for all police officers and managers in relation to issues of ethnicity and race. There is a national BPA, as well as a growing number of force BPAs.
CSO	Community Support Officer.
HMIC	Her Majesty's Inspectorate of Constabulary. A body of senior people (some of them retired chief constables) appointed by the Crown who inspect police forces and publish reports on what they find. There is a Chief Inspector of Constabulary who oversees the work of regional offices. Some Inspectors have a very specific function—such as training.
LAGPA	Gay Police Association. Provides support and advice for all police officers and managers in relation to relevant issues.
MFH	Missing from home.
NCIS	National Criminal Intelligence Service. Made up of seconded police officers, customs officers and many others. Responsible for monitoring criminals and crime on a national basis. Work out of regional offices with a main office in London. Soon to be allowed to recruit its own police officers.
NCPE	National Centre for Policing Excellence.

NCS	National Crime Squad. Organisation responsible for investigating major crime on a national basis. Work out of regional offices with a main office in London. Soon to be allowed to recruit its own police officers.
PITO	Police Information Technology Organisation.
Police Federation	Like the police officers' trade union (at least for officers of the ranks from constable up to chief inspector). Set up under an Act of Parliament, the Federation has regional offices across England and Wales and a national office in Surrey. Each force has a number of Federation representatives who are elected by its members. They will provide advice on aspects of welfare, conditions of service, discipline and health and safety.
PSU	Police Standards Unit. This Unit provides guidance at a strategic level to police forces on maintaining standards.
Superintendents' Association	Similar to the Federation but for Superintendents and Chief Superintendents.

Expression	*Meaning*
ABH	Actual bodily harm—an offence under section 47 of the Offences Against the Person Act 1861. Generally involves fairly high degree of injury like lost tooth and bad bruising. See also section 47 and OAP.
ACC	Assistant Chief Constable.
ACR	Area control room (a large room full of computers, telephones, radio equipment and lots of key people—officers' lifeline).
AFIS	Automated fingerprint identification system.

ANPR	Automated Number Plate Recognition system.
Appropriate adult	Every person under 17 who is in custody or being interviewed requires the assistance of an appropriate adult. Usually a parent or guardian but not necessarily. Also required by other vulnerable people in custody such as people with mental difficulties.
APS	Acting police sergeant. Applies to other ranks as well, e.g. A/CI = acting chief inspector.
ARV	Armed response vehicle.
ASBO	Anti-social behaviour order. Order passed by the magistrates' or county court to stop people whose behaviour is making their neighbours' lives miserable. The police and local authority can apply for them.
BCU	Basic command unit (a large police station).
Brief	A lawyer representing defendant or a warrant card.
C&D	Complaints and discipline department. Same as D&C and (below).
CDRP	Crime and Disorder Reduction Partnerships—set up under the Crime and Disorder Act 1998. It includes local authorities, fire authorities, health authorities and the police.
CHIS	Covert human intelligence source (informant).
CIS	Crime information/intelligence system.
CJSU	Criminal justice support unit. Department responsible for managing proposed prosecution files and related matters. The first 'end user' of your paperwork! See also CJU.
CJU	Criminal justice unit—same as CJSU.
Club number	See CRO number.
Con & Use	The Road Vehicles (Construction and Use)

Regulations. Amended all the time and contain masses of useful detail about vehicles such as how much tread they have to have on their tyres, what sort of condition they have to be in etc. and less useful bits such as the requirements of motorised hedge trimmers and whether trailers carrying round timber are exempt from having mudflaps.

CRO number Criminal Records Office number. Every convicted person gets allocated one of these. Recorded on PNC; see also Club number.

D&C Discipline and complaints department—the people who deal with discipline and complaints against police officers. The department who will serve the Reg 9 form (see below). Often part of the professional standards or misconduct unit; see also C&D and CIB.

Dep Deputy Chief Constable—often acts as a Chief Constable while the Chief's away.

DNA Deoxyribonucleic acid (see why it's just called DNA?) Gene identification. Found in hair, semen and other samples that are taken from suspects or recovered from crime scenes.

DPA Data Protection Act (covers what you can and can't do with people's personal details recorded at work).

DSU Divisional support unit (a van full of police officers); see also MSU and PSU.

D&D Drunk and disorderly. The offence committed where someone is disorderly while drunk in a public place.

Due care Driving without due care and attention. Probably

	the most common motoring offence. Includes everything from ignoring road signs to driving through puddles and splashing pedestrians.
Egress	Normally used in crime reports to refer to the way a criminal got out of a building. Egress is the opposite of 'entry' and often criminals use a different way out from the way they got in.
HORT/1	Home Office Road Traffic 1 form—also known as a producer, this is the piece of paper that officers give to motorists allowing them seven days to produce their driving documents at a police station of their choice.
IO	Investigating officer (usually in an internal police investigation).
IP	Injured party or person (victim).
MO	*Modus operandi.* The method of operating used by a particular criminal (e.g. always wears a mask, kicks in kitchen door, etc.).
MOP	Member of the public.
MSU	Mobile support unit (a van full of police officers— sometimes known as 'Black Maria' after some wicked Victorian felon); see also DSU and PSU.
NFA	'No further action' (method of writing off police calls or tasks) or 'no fixed abode'.
NIM	National Intelligence Model. A system for gathering and using criminal intelligence.
NIP	Notice of Intended Prosecution. Notice (oral or in writing) that you have to give motorists before reporting them for certain road traffic offences (such as speeding) within 14 days unless they have had an accident at the time.
OAP	Offences Against the Person Act 1861 (could be

	Old Age Piece of legislation. Sounds ancient—and is. Still applies to most assaults today); see sections 18, 20, 39 and 47.
OPL	Over the prescribed limit (driving whilst . . .). See also Poz alco.
PI	Participating informant—person (non-police) who has been authorised to play a limited part in criminal activity in order to catch offenders; see also CHIS. Can also stand for police inspector.
PII	Public interest immunity—legal expression whereby the police and others apply to a court to prevent documents or other evidence from being used, usually because it would pose a threat to public interest (e.g. because an informant is named in the document, etc.)
PNC	Police National Computer. Contains details of all people with criminal convictions, etc. See also CRO and CRO number.
Poz alco	Positive alcohol—driving while over the prescribed alcohol limit. See also OPL.
PSU	Police support unit (vans full of police officers, usually two sergeants plus 20 constables); see also DSU and MSU. Do not confuse with Policing Standards Unit.
Reg 9	Form that is served on police officers (under Regulation 9 of the Police (Conduct) Regulations 1999) warning them that they are being investigated for possible criminal/conduct offences. Used to be called Reg 7s; see also D&C and C&D.
Reg 7	See Reg 9.
SOCO	Scenes of crime office/officer. Technical department which specialises in collecting,

packaging and examining evidence found at the scene of crimes. Excellent source of advice for many things such as preservation of evidence and 'bagging and tagging' exhibits.

SIO
Senior investigating officer, usually senior detective working on major enquiry such as murder or abduction.

Section 4
Offence of putting person in fear of unlawful violence (Public Order Act 1986.)

Section 5
Offence of using threatening, abusive or insulting words or behaviour (Public Order Act 1986).

Section 25
The general arrest conditions set out under the Police and Criminal Evidence Act 1984 (PACE). They allow police officers to arrest someone for virtually any offence but only if one of the conditions applies. Often thought (wrongly) to mean a power of arrest if the suspect refuses to give their name and address—it's much more sophisticated than that.

Section 29 production
Power to allow prisoners out of custody so that they can help the police with enquiries into other offences. Taken from section 29 of the Criminal Justice Act 1961.

Section 47
An offence under section 47 of the Offences Against the Person Act 1861—actual bodily harm—generally involves fairly high degree of injury like a lost tooth and bad bruising. See also ABH and OAP.

Section 136
The power to remove people from public places if they appear to be suffering from a mental disorder. Taken from the Mental Health Act 1983.

Skipper
Sergeant (usually heard in South East England).

Super	Superintendent.
TDA	Offence of 'taking and driving away' (Theft Act 1968, section 12). Referred to in newspapers as 'joyriding'. See also UTMV, TWOC and TWLA.
TWLA	Offence of 'taking without lawful authority' (Theft Act 1968, section 12). Referred to in newspapers as 'joyriding'. See also UTMV, TDA and TWOC.
TWOC	Offence of taking conveyance without the owner's consent (Theft Act 1968, section 12). Referred to in newspapers as 'joyriding'. See also UTMV, TDA and TWLA.
UTMV	Offence of unlawful taking of motor vehicle (Theft Act 1968, section 12). Referred to in newspapers as 'joyriding'. See also TWOC, TDA and TWLA.

Radio communication

Much police communication is done via the radio network, a network that is getting better and smarter all the time. Each patrol officer has a personal radio which they are trained how to use when they get to their particular force. Each force uses what is referred to as the '10 Code'. This involves abbreviating more common messages into a coded format beginning with the number 10. So, '10 four' may mean that a message has been received and understood, or '10 twelve' may mean that the officer has made an arrest. The 10 Code is used for brevity and security and officers/radio operators will learn the main codes when they receive their radio training. Because it becomes such a part of everyday life, the 10 Code is often used in casual conversation by some officers *when they're not using the radio*!

One thing that police officers and other personnel need to get to grips with is the phonetic alphabet. This is particularly useful when you are trying to give the spelling of a word over the radio or telephone. You must have come across call centre staff or telesales people who ask you *'is that "F" for Freddy?'* or *'do you mean "A" for Apple?'* Well, this is what the phonetic alphabet does—except that the words used are agreed in advance and everyone uses the same words so that people don't have to rack their brains for something that begins with 'Q' or 'W'. That's the good news; the bad news is that some of them are a bit odd and don't immediately spring to mind in everyday life, like Foxtrot (a quaint ballroom dance) or Lima (the capital of Peru). You may have heard the American version used in films and TV programmes. If you have, you can forget most of them because they are different from the UK ones.

The phonetic alphabet as used by the UK police, other emergency services and armed forces is as follows:

A	Alpha	B	Bravo	C	Charlie	D	Delta
E	Echo	F	Foxtrot	G	Golf	H	Hotel
I	India	J	Juliet	K	Kilo	L	Lima
M	Mike	N	November	O	Oscar	P	Papa
Q	Quebec	R	Romeo	S	Sierra	T	Tango
U	Uniform	V	Victor	W	Whisky	X	X-Ray
Y	Yankee	Z	Zulu				

As with the caution, it is worth learning these sooner rather than later (and these really *do* crop up in quiz programmes). The Scottish spelling 'whisky' here is deliberate but not compulsory. Oscar Kilo?

FURTHER READING

Clements & Spinks, *The Equal Opportunities Guide*, London: Kogan Page.

APPENDIX

An example of a Probationer Training Programme*

The Probationer Training Programme is an agreement between forces and the Police Training Council to provide a consistent national training programme. The probationary period lasts two years in which time you will need to demonstrate your competence to become a police officer. The programme is a mixture of practical policing and training, but the main focus will be on training and development.

Stage One will be conducted at Headquarters to provide an induction into the Police Service, as well as presenting a general introduction to policing issues.

Stage Two will be delivered at a Police Training Centre (PTC) and contain the required theoretical knowledge with opportunities to apply learning in simulations. During Stage Two core policing skills will be developed as well as the supporting knowledge and understanding.

Stage Three is undertaken at your Headquarters allowing you to extend knowledge gained from the PTC and place it in a force context. Where appropriate, issues relating to local procedures will be delivered during this stage.

Stage Four is a practically-based phase consisting of street patrol and other relevant attachments supervised by a personal tutor.

Stage Five consists of further in-force training at Headquarters to include those subjects in the syllabus not previously covered and prepares you for independent patrol.

*Courtesy of South Wales Police

Stage six will give you the opportunity to undertake independent patrol, when you will need to demonstrate your ability to work with little direct supervision. In addition, Stage Six includes a minimum of 20 days' training to support your development. At the end of this period the final decision will be made, again based on the evidence contained in your PDP, as to your suitability to become a proficient police officer. Reaching this stage is no guarantee that you will be considered suitable and serious consideration is given as to whether you will be an asset or a very expensive liability to the police service. Obviously the assessment system is designed so that any problem areas have been recognised by both you and the organisation prior to this, so you will already be aware of any points which may affect the outcome of the decision making process.

It should be emphasised that the Probationer Training Programme is currently a two-year training period and you will be continually assessed during the whole period. As discussed in the previous chapters, learning does not end there but your probationary development forms the foundation for your future career development.

As you can see, assessments written by you and about you form a very important part of your training.

Let's look at what is required in the self-assessment.

Creativity and innovation

Seeks new ways of doing things, with the notion of continuous improvement in mind. Has an open-minded attitude to new ideas and ways of working. Constructively questions procedures and suggests improvements, helping to implement changes.

These five core skills will be implemented into core tasks, each of which contains several subheadings and are listed blow.

Core tasks

Unit 1 – Patrolling
1.1   Planning a beat
1.2   Patrolling a beat

Unit 2 – Investigating

2.1   Initial investigation of crime

2.2   Supporting victims and witnesses

Unit 3 – Arresting

3.1   Making arrests

3.2   Escorting detainees

3.3   Searching

3.4   Interview—planning

3.5   Conducting interviews

3.6   Searching land, premises and property

3.7   Gathering and evaluating evidence

3.8   Case papers; documentation and court proceedings

Unit 4 – Dealing with incidents and disputes

4.1   Incidents

4.2   Disputes

Unit 5 – Dealing with traffic

5.1   Motoring Offences

5.2   Road Traffic Accidents

5.3   Drink Drive

Unit 6 – In the police station

6.1   Front Office—enquiry desk

6.2   The custody suite—gaoler

The core skills and tasks will be explained more fully in-force and will be supplemented by the National Occupational Standards.

The current probationary period

The probationary period lasts for two years, divided into stages.

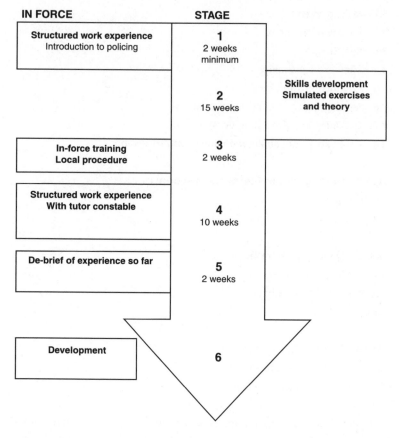

Please note that this model is under review and may change significantly in 2004.

Metropolitan Police Service: The initial training programme*

Eighteen weeks, with 10 themes including a written and practical assessment on each throughout the course. These themes are:

- policing London in the right way
- becoming an investigator
- work traffic, think crime
- patrolling effectively
- managing crime scenes and suspects
- policing for a diverse community
- preparing for a successful prosecution
- reducing road casualties
- responding to victims
- working for a safer community.

The core skills you will develop are:

- Decision-making—gathering all relevant information, checking for accuracy, applying your knowledge and maintaining objectivity.
- Self motivation – showing an interest in your work, perseverance, seeking new challenges and striving to meet deadlines.
- Communication—being articulate and fluent when speaking, adapting your communication style to your audience, listening actively, asking probing questions to clarify understanding, and writing clear, logically structured reports.
- Professional standards—being sensitive to the needs and feelings of others, being supportive to colleagues, consulting others, staying calm and confident under stress, and looking at a situation from others' points of view.
- Integrity—displaying your trustworthiness and compassion, and, challenging inappropriate behaviour at all times.

* Courtesy of the MPS.

INDEX